Arthur Shepherd

AMERICAN COMPOSER

To Dick Loucks
my heartiest
June 6, 1955

Arthur Shepherd

AMERICAN COMPOSER

RICHARD LOUCKS

BRIGHAM YOUNG
UNIVERSITY PRESS

Library of Congress Cataloging in Publication Data

Loucks, Richard, 1919–
Arthur Shepherd, American composer.

Bibliography: p. 247
1. Shepherd, Arthur, 1880–1958. 2. Composers—United States—Biography. I. Title.
ML410.S525L7 780'.92'4 [B] 79-22143
ISBN 0-8425-1706-5

International Standard Book Number: 0-8425-1706-5
Brigham Young University Press, Provo, Utah 84602

Printed in the United States of America
80 .5Mc 38879

To

Grazella Shepherd and Marian Loucks

If one must pick and choose, I'll put it this way: J. S. Bach is my first love, but my favorite composer is Bahaymobeeschub.

Work, work, work—it becomes almost a mania with me these days. Is there any better medicine or Anodyne?

Change of Tactics! The Spirit rather than the letter!

Don't analyze until you have to, but when you have to you should know how.

Let's *simplify* and move ahead!

How does music make sense?

Arthur Shepherd

CONTENTS

FOREWORD

The invitation to write this foreword comes twenty-one long years after Arthur Shepherd's death in early 1958 and only a few short weeks after the death of his second wife (from 1922), Grazella P. Shepherd. But my memory of a close, influential association with those two wonderful people, especially during Arthur's last three decades, remains as fresh as ever. Now, after reading the draft of Professor Loucks's fine book, the memory almost becomes the reality once more. Indeed, thanks to his modest and unassuming yet highly perceptive approach, his eschewal of superfluous scholarship, his honest emphasis on what matters in art and life, and his large and tolerant views, the reader can be assured of a book that is peculiarly in tune with its subject—with both the man and the musician.

My own article in *The Musical Quarterly* for 1950, to which Professor Loucks refers, was a preliminary effort to report on Shepherd and his music. More recently, the late F. Karl Grossman—who worked in Shepherd's sphere over a long period—chronicled many of the events in which Shepherd shared (as well as providing two fine photographs of him) in *A History of Music in Cleveland* (Cleveland: Case Western Reserve University, 1972). With the publication of Professor Loucks's book, perhaps the one additional contribution that I could offer in this foreword would be a small number of my own recollections that seem especially characteristic of Shepherd.

Arthur and Grazella shared, with an ever-fresh delight, an idyllic life in the lovely Blossom home made available to them throughout most of their Cleveland years. When it had to be withdrawn from them abruptly and unexpectedly in their last years together, Arthur in particular, who had been able to accept disappointments in his career so philosophically, found it very hard to accept the loss of their privacy and space, and their favorite trees, flowers, and birds, to be cooped in an apartment.

For all his acute penetration of the arts Shepherd was no effete aesthete. When nearly seventy he was invited to conduct the [University of North] Carolina Choir in a program of his choral works. We got ready to drive into Chapel Hill for the first rehearsal and found my car battery dead; thereupon he proposed and evidently relished riding in on the back of my huge Harley-Davidson motorcycle—so much so that he insisted on doing it again for the next rehearsal.

When Shepherd got started on a new composition, lecture, or related project, he quickly became totally involved. Any unavoidable distraction found him preoccupied and nervously chafing to return to the project. It was at such a time that my Ph.D. orals happened to be scheduled—a circumstance that could have made them a "breeze" for me had it not been for the other members of the committee he was chairing, who were equally critical but less preoccupied. I had the good fortune to be serving as his graduate assistant while he was composing his Second Symphony; the result was almost total involvement on my part as well as his. Among other things, he asked me to prepare a four-hand piano arrangement as the scoring progressed, but like Beethoven with Moscheles and *Fidelio,* he found good reason to improve and complete the arrangement himself. We played it over and over (until he must have had it memorized) so that he could evaluate it in live sound and motion before handing it over to the Cleveland Symphony Orchestra for its first performance. The opportunity to observe so closely the gestation process and the excruciating self-criticism—especially in a work that I found to be increasingly convincing in both its materials and their handling—was invaluable.

Shepherd stood second to none of his contemporaries in his professional craftsmanship, but Professor Loucks is justified in writing of his excessive self-criticism at times. As late as 1950, while Shepherd was coaching me prior to further performances of his admirable Second Piano Sonata (originally published in 1930), I found myself almost jealously trying to preserve the status quo of the score against his onslaught of newly proposed changes. (My score had benefited already from all the understandable pruning made for the second edition of 1951.) For a fine, authentic performance of that work available today, the reader can refer to the recording by Vivien Harvey Slater, which must have come as close as any to satisfying Shepherd's ideal. It was not released until 1967, as Professor Loucks explains.

An unusual involvement for Shepherd—and for any daily paper in a large city—was his intellectual embroilment in the *Cleveland Press*'s column of letters. For several months he maintained a running battle in defense of three-measure and other "irregular" phrases as valid entities and not simply four-measure phrases contracted or expanded. He was fighting a strong surviving contingent of Hugo Riemann-ites and their belief in the "square phrase." I mean to dig up that correspondence some time, for it involved several of Cleveland's most prominent musicians. After nearly fifty years I can recall with certainty only that Beryl Rubinstein was among the participants, probably on Shepherd's side. There could have been no victorious side, but I can remember one of Shepherd's prime evidences (quoted right in the column, if memory serves) as the opening of Schubert's "Great Symphony in C." It is no wonder that Shepherd fought that battle so vigorously. At times, "irregular" phrases occupied him almost obsessively in his composing. He worried considerably, too, about choosing the irregular barring most appropriate to those phrases—one reason why Copland came to interest him so much. In spite of all his experience as a conductor, such barring brought him temporary defeat when he started to rehearse the Cleveland Symphony Orchestra for that first performance of his Second Symphony. Artur Rodzinsky, listening from the hall, tried his hand at conducting this barring and held the group together a little better. But ultimately Shepherd agreed to convert whole sections to regular barring and to let the phrases, adequately defined by other markings, fall where they might. The improvement in ensemble was overwhelming, and Shepherd took the experience as a most edifying lesson.

Finally, I never remember Shepherd happier than when he was making music, especially intimate chamber music among friends with whom he could then review the experience and reactions. Among those with whom he most seemed to enjoy making music was the front-rank "amateur" violinist Jerome Gross. Gross was a jocular, robust, indefatigable phenomenon (see the picture in Grossman's book) who performed important surgery twelve hours a day and practiced or played violin the other twelve. The two men played Shepherd's Sonata for Pianoforte and Violin several times in public. No one who attended one such performance, at the Cleveland Museum of Art, will ever forget what surely must have been one of the most extended instances of Alphonse-and-Gastonism in all of music history. They dallied not only to determine who should go on stage first but, again, who should go off first—all in full view of the greatly amused audience. Shepherd and Gross themselves laughed—and argued—long and hard over the experience afterwards.

William S. Newman
University of North Carolina
at Chapel Hill

PREFACE

I am certain that valuable books have been written because their authors realized that no one else would tackle the job. I claim no special competence, but only patience and determination. There is no dearth of persons who knew Arthur Shepherd well, who can "see" his music with clear vision, and whose powers of expression are fitted to the task this book represents. These pages were written in my spare time over a number of years—not a superior but, nevertheless, an unavoidable method. To the best of my knowledge it is accurate in factual information; yet there remains much in Shepherd's life of which I am unaware. To the best of my ability I have described his skill and his music with insights drawn from long study; yet my thoughts are inevitably colored by my own musical nature. A man is at the mercy of his biographer. I hope that my understanding of music and of Shepherd will lead others to his work, and I pray that nothing I have written will turn others from him. This book exists because I wanted his name on it, not mine. I persuaded myself that it should be written now, while firsthand acquaintance with him still exists and before his manuscripts are lost or destroyed. I believe that Shepherd's music possesses the vitality to endure, and I consider my effort well spent.

In studying Shepherd's music one is faced with a variety of forms and expressive traits. On the one hand there are at least five classes of music: works for orchestra, pieces for chamber ensembles, piano pieces, choral works, and solo songs with piano or orchestral accompaniment. Second, there are identifiable differences between early and late works, differences that arise from the gradual development of his aesthetics and intentions as he experienced the artistic turmoil that transformed musical style during the span of his own creative life. Third, one can trace the development of his techniques of harmony, counterpoint, texture, and form.

In an earlier dissertation (University of Rochester, 1960) I attempted to describe each of these facets in detail as well as many of the interrelationships among them. This turned out to be an organizational and analytical project of such immensity as to impair practical use of the work. Later I reduced the dissertation to the manageable proportions of some 400 pages; but, like its forerunner, this volume remained a description of Shepherd's life and music, interlaced with a large number of examples and excerpts from his scores. The reduction, however, left me dissatisfied. Though I had produced a scholarly study that would place Shepherd, for our time, in the literature about twentieth-century music, I could not convince myself that I had labored in the best interests of his music, and I was certain that the numerous pages of technical description and analysis would bore many whom I wanted to reach. I am, frankly, more interested in those who, having read my book, might be moved to play the music than in those who would seek merely information. Besides, I became more certain, the more I read those pages, that persons interested in such detail would probably prefer to work it out for themselves. Furthermore, the publication of a hundred or more pages of excerpts and fragments from Shepherd's compositions seemed particularly wasteful, for it left the reader as dependent as before on the few published compositions available.

I was fortunate to have in Howard Webber the most sympathetic and helpful of editors. I do not know whether he knew a way out and gently guided me toward the answer, or whether he merely encouraged an almost random thought as we discussed this problem one day. But that is no matter. What is important is that he was willing to endure patiently my dawdling and bumbling for another year while I worked it out. Although he could not, in the end, publish the revision, his role in its coming about was still vital. The purposes of this book, therefore, are to present in facsimile many of Shepherd's unpublished compositions and to enhance them, for those who are interested, with a biography and analysis of his compositional methods. It may seem curious that I have illustrated most of my points by reference to obscure rather than well-known works. But all the works are discussed in one way or another, and the dissertation mentioned is available for those who need fuller coverage.

The dates of compositions have been included in the text at the first mention of a work, or whenever the date is necessary for clarification or for identification of the composition. The dates of all works are also given in Appendix A. An asterisk (*) identifies scores reproduced in this volume.

My thanks for the help given me extends in many directions: to Grazella Shepherd, the composer's wife, and Marian Kirk Loucks, my wife, who made my work possible and to whom it is dedicated; to the composer's brother Harry Shepherd; to William S. Newman; to Edward G. Evans, Jr.; and to the staffs of the Western Reserve Historical Society, the Freiberger Library of Case Western Reserve University, and the Marriott Library of Fine Arts at the University of Utah—and particularly, in the latter case, to Everett L. Cooley and Della L. Dye. For financial support I am indebted to my parents, Zeke Brunson Loucks and Richard N. Loucks, Jr.; to Pomona College, Claremont, California; and to Case Western Reserve University, Cleveland, Ohio. Finally, I express appreciation to my reviewers, to my editors David Dalton and Elizabeth Wilkinson, and to others of the staff of Brigham Young University Press whose confidence in and hard work on this project have brought it to fruition.

In addition, acknowledgment is due a number of individuals and organizations for their kind permission to use previously published materials. Quotes from the Budge history of Paris, Idaho, are used by courtesy of Helen Budge Folland. Excerpts from the Arthur Shepherd articles published in the *Proceedings of the Music Educators National Conference* are used by permission of the MENC. The Olin Downes review, copyright 1950 by The New York Times Company, is reprinted by permission. Oxford University Press has kindly granted permission for the use of the materials quoted from W. W. Cobbett, Donald Francis Tovey, W. H. Hadow, and H. K. Hadley. Excerpts from articles by Arthur Shepherd and William S. Newman are used by permission of *The Musical Quarterly.*

Program notes of the Cleveland Orchestra are excerpted by permission of the Cleveland Orchestra. Permission to reproduce the musical excerpt from *Horizons* was granted by Summy-Birchard Music, and permission to reproduce *Reverie* by New Valley Music Press of Smith College. A stanza from the poem "Virgil" from *Others to Adorn* by Oliver St. John Gogarty, published by Rich and Cowan, appears by arrangement. The lyrics of "Spinning Song" by Edith Sitwell appear by permission of Vanguard Press, Incorporated. The words of "Sarasvati" are reprinted by permission of Macmillan Publishing Company, Incorporated, from *Collected Poems* of James Stephens; copyright 1931 by Macmillan Publishing Company, Incorporated, renewed 1959 by Cynthia Stephens.

Richard Loucks
Professor of Music
Pomona College

PART ONE:

PARIS, IDAHO, TO BOSTON

CHAPTER 1

PARIS: 1880–1892

Paris, Idaho!? (there must have been a *humorist* at the christening). What is it like? I can best describe what it *was* like as my birthplace and my home until my 17th year. A village, some 35 or 40 miles over the Utah borderline, in the Bear Lake valley settled by pioneer Mormon converts mostly of British lineage. Enchanting country, rugged mountainous terrain on the west; wide fertile fields, farms, meadows on the east and on the south, the Bear Lake probably one of the loveliest of its kind in the Rocky Mountain region; as colorful as Lake Tahoe.[1]

Among American composers of his generation—and, indeed, we may include even the generation before him—Arthur Shepherd is distinguished by the seeming unlikeliness of his origins. Paris was virtually a frontier town even as late as his birth on February 19, 1880. "Cowboys, Indians and miners were familiar apparitions in the local scene; but they were more than apparitions; all the real stuff."[2]

Paris had been settled in 1863 when the region was still a frontier. It is vividly described by Jesse R. S. Budge, a boyhood friend of Shepherd, in his book, *Pioneer Days—Some Reminiscences.*[3]

It was, like most Mormon communities, located near a mountain stream—Paris Creek—from which water was diverted for irrigation of small farms and gardens. Some of the cabins had dirt floors and most were one, two or three-room structures made of logs with small windows.

Clothing and furniture were homemade and a bed tick filled with straw served as a mattress. It was in this Mormon town that Arthur's father and mother were married in 1877, and in which they established their home.

William N. B. Shepherd, Arthur's father, was born in Southampton, England, on September 18, 1854. William's brother, Joseph R., in discussing his family's life in England, writes:

It was at Brockenhurst that Elder William Budge, then a traveling elder of the "Mormon" church, stopped at my father's humble home, and became quite closely associated with my parents. I have often heard my mother speak with considerable satisfaction of the little services that she rendered Brother Budge, by mending his clothes, and ministering to his other wants at this time. It seems that there were two or three "Mormon" families living at Brockenhurst. . . . Little did either my parents or brother Budge at this time think, that in later times their lives and lots should be so closely associated.

Later passages refer to William and his fiancee, who was to be Arthur's mother, and their departure for America.

It was while at Fawley that my brother William made the acquaintance of a young lady by the name of Emily Mary Phipps [*sic:* the name is Phipp], to whom he became engaged, and subsequently married after reaching Paris, Idaho, in America. . . .

In the autumn of the year 1877, after disposing of all their household effects, and fitting out with the requisite conveniences for the trip, father and mother, with all of their children excepting Angie, who was then living with her husband, John Norton, at Southampton, accompanied by a Miss Emily M. Phipps [*sic*], fiancée of my brother William, bade adieu to friends and acquaintents [*sic*], and the village of Fawley, and started upon the journey to America.[4]

William was a man of strict integrity and independent character, with an inherent ability to make a living from the opportunities he encountered in the new country. He was a photographer and an accountant, with marked artistic and musical interests. He also developed an interest in public affairs that led him to serve as a justice of the peace and eventually as a member of the Idaho State Legislature. In 1897 he moved his family to Salt Lake City. He was still active in 1944 when, at the age of ninety, a reporter described him as "the little, white-haired man with the impish smile and sparkling wit."[5] He had become so skilled in watercolor painting, which was his hobby, that he had attained some prominence in Salt Lake City art circles. He died in 1945.

Emily Mary Phipp Shepherd, to whom Arthur bore a striking physical resemblance, was a woman of strong mentality and moral character. Born at Ware, near London, she was the same age as her husband. Like him she was musical, and as a young woman she loved to sing. She bore nine sons and a daughter: William, Arthur, Henry (Harry), Walter, Nathaniel, Ralph, Septimus, Charles, Albert, and Josephine. Three became musicians: Arthur a composer, Charles a pianist, and Albert a violinist.

By the time Arthur was born in 1880, living conditions in Paris were no longer primitive, though the area remained relatively isolated until the Union Pacific and Oregon Shortline reached Montpelier, Idaho, in about 1882. Jesse Budge wrote:

> Of course, those of my generation did not experience the severe hardships which the first settlers, or even our parents endured. Our early years constituted the fringe, so to speak, of pioneer days, the period of transition from days of real want and hardship to those in which the necessities, but practically no luxuries, were obtainable; a period when there were no rich and none entirely destitute, and when self-reliance, industry and integrity gave assurance of a measure of success and prosperity. There was very little leisure time so far as I can now recall, for every season of the year required the performance of seasonable service.[6]

In spite of hardships, the family was happy and the children's lives full of fun and laughter. In the days of his retirement in Cleveland, Shepherd tingled with delight as he recounted the Fourth of July celebrations and other joyful occasions in Paris:

> The town band always played from the roof of the courthouse. Firecrackers were not noisy enough; we used shotguns. And for some even shotguns were too tame. It was one of the Rich boys, I think, who set off a stick of dynamite one year way back there. It blew up the bridge in the middle of town. . . . We used to ride in wagons to Bear Lake, about fifteen miles from Paris, for our picnics. It was such a beautiful lake, blue like Donner and Tahoe in the Sierras. There were always games, and on the way home there was invariably a wagon race.[7]

Later Shepherd wrote that his boyhood "was of a kind to stimulate physical activity and right thinking."[8] He loved country life; his early familiarity with the outdoors instilled in him a profound reverence for nature that would later inspire some of his best music.

Music was, of course, homemade. As Jesse Budge remembered:

> When a very small boy I was a member of the Paris fife and drum band conducted by L. T. (Tracy) Shepherd and later for three or four years I played successively 3rd, 2nd, and then 1st cornet in the Paris brass band conducted by Joseph R. Shepherd. When employed in the hayfield, on "The Island" about 8 miles distant from Paris, I would ride home on horseback, once a week—every Thursday evening—for band practice, and leave for the ranch early enough the next morning to be ready for work.
>
> When my voice had changed, I became a member of the Bear Lake Stake Choir, conducted by W. N. B. Shepherd . . . and later by Joseph R. Shepherd.[9]

Among the many benefits brought by the new railroad, the availability of reed organs and pianos is of particular importance to this story, for this made possible not only the discovery but the early development of Arthur's talent. "Uncle Joe" (Joseph R. Shepherd) loved to drop by Arthur's home after work, where together they would read through the popular songs of the day.

> As a youngster music was in the household, by way of a reed-organ, but more *important*: the singing of English glees by uncles born in England. I early learned to read at sight: *how* I have never known. Still more important, in my early teens, or possibly before, some nice woman presented me with a volume of Beethoven Sonatas. That probably set me going.[10]

Although the active musical life, professional musicians, and other appurtenances of music in a large cultural center were lacking in Paris, we can easily understand that in such a musical family Arthur's talent was noticed and appreciated. Fortunately, his family was also willing to provide him with the instruction necessary to develop his musical gifts. In a letter to William S. Newman Arthur describes the crucial decision his family made in his musical education:

> How did I get to Boston in 1892? Well following my first real music teacher, George Haessel (a fine sturdy German, or Swiss) then I continued instruction, locally, under Otto Haenisch, who gave me some notions of keyboard technique and fed me on good classical literature. He persuaded my father to send me to a reputable music school. It was a close decision, as between Leipzig and Boston. In consideration of my tender years (12) Boston was decided upon. Shortly before my graduation (with honors) in 1897, my family had moved to Salt Lake City, so that became my home. There I taught, played, and began composing.[11]

Shepherd family at home in Paris, Idaho. Arthur is seated on the gatepost.

BOSTON: 1892–1897

The twelve-year-old Arthur journeyed to Boston in the company of Dr. Ezra Rich and Dr. Edward I. Rich, both of whom were honeymooning. These sons of an early settler of Paris placed him in the hands of a group of men from Utah then in residence at Harvard University. One of these, John Widtsoe, settled the boy into the first of several boarding houses that were to be his homes in the coming years and introduced him to the authorities at the New England Conservatory. Shepherd related that he lived at this time with "a gang of boys." They were in the habit of pasting their extra pennies in the form of a star on a bulletin board. Later in the month when they were about out of money, they would pry off the pennies and buy food.

One can imagine the impression that musical Boston must have made on this naive, eager listener. In 1923, during a discussion of the Cleveland Orchestra's Children's Concerts before the Music Supervisors National Conference, he said:

Our audiences in Cleveland are drawn mainly from the grade schools, reaching children of an average age of 12. It was my own good fortune to hear a symphony orchestra for the first time at about this age. It was the Boston Symphony, with Nikisch conducting, and the symphony was the fifth of Beethoven. To describe the effect of that mighty motive, the sheer impact of vibration and rhythm to those four notes, would require more eloquence than I possess. Revert, for yourselves to the first time you had a similar experience—and reflect upon its significance in your life.[12]

Arthur was a fine student, but he did not grind at his lessons. Sometimes, "when I should have been practicing," he played hooky and went to a baseball game. He gained a reputation for sight-reading that put him in demand for ensemble playing. He traveled with a small concert company that performed in the towns about Boston, and for a while he played with an orchestra in the Castle Square Hotel. Summers he returned to Paris for vacation and the renewal of family ties. His transcript lists his courses and teachers, but since it ignores composition with Percy Goetschius, the list may be incomplete.

1892–93	
Piano	Edward D. Hale
Solfege	Samuel W. Cole
Hand Culture	Mrs. C. F. Nichols
1893–94	
Piano	Charles F. Dennée
Harmony	Benjamin Cutter
Theory	Louis C. Elson
1894–95	
Piano	Charles F. Dennée
Harmony	Percy Goetschius
1895–96	
Piano	Carl Faelten
Harmony	Percy Goetschius
Sightreading	Reinhold Faelten
Counterpoint	Percy Goetschius
1896–97	
Piano	Carl Faelten
Composition	George W. Chadwick
Ensemble	Leo Schultz

His relations with his teachers seem to have been close. Arthur had a natural talent for the piano, and he was particularly influenced by Charles Dennée, whose advanced keyboard technique won his respect, and by Carl Faelten, with whom he seems to have been especially congenial. For Benjamin Cutter the adult Shepherd revealed deep affection, describing him as a man of magnetic personality and charm, a student and critic of both contemporary and classic works, and an enthusiastic as well as talented teacher of harmony. In his final year Arthur studied composition with George W. Chadwick, whom he described as an independent, virile, American spirit and a self-confident, peppery man of great charm. Nevertheless, in references to his conservatory days, he invariably revealed his greater loyalty to Percy Goetschius for guidance in creative work.

Shepherd was in attendance at the New England Conservatory at the time of the factional dissensions that resulted in the separation of Faelten and Goetschius from the faculty and the appointment of Chadwick as director. He usually discussed the matter in terms of its results rather than of the issues or personalities. "Musical Boston was, in effect, an outpost of German musical culture,"[13] but Chadwick symbolized, in his person and in his talents, a turn toward a new order in American musical education. Under the leadership of this composer, whose outstanding talents had won recognition abroad as well as in the United States, a fresh, American spirit and outlook could develop at the conservatory. Chadwick's elevation was an early instance of the assumption by American musicians of posts commensurate with their abilities.

Percy Goetschius, with whom Shepherd cherished a lifelong friendship, exerted the greatest influence upon the boy. The Shepherd Collection[14] today contains a bundle of Goetschius's letters, spanning almost half a century from 1901 to 1942, in which one can trace the ever-growing respect and admiration that developed between the two men. In an article following Goetschius's death in 1943, Shepherd recounted the pedagogue's contributions to American music and included testimonials from other students of that distinguished gentleman:

> In the old Conservatory corridors in Boston, no single personage was more symbolic of the *fin de siècle* cultural pattern than "Doctor" Percy Goetschius. On first encounter, one was a bit overawed by the professional austerity: the bespectacled visage, the intellectual brow, the closely cropped beard, and the bony frame united to create a type that our provincial fancy had never before associated with a musical personality. In due time, however, one caught up with the realization that here indeed was a scholar-musician whose every gesture was in harmony with his vocation. Likewise, one came to relish the scrupulous English diction that he used on the lecture platform, a diction that had a kind of Mendelssohnian grace even when he was dealing with matters seemingly arid and remote. If the lectures in history were more attractive in manner than in matter, the analytical talks, introductory to recital performances in Sleeper Hall, brought flashes of enthusiasm that overcame any tendency towards apathy in the student body.
>
> With such a musician on the staff, there was never a suspicion of lag in the educational enterprises of the old school. If there was some chamber-music masterpiece to be introduced, the adroit analyst was at hand with his ready keyboard illustrations; if the orchestral part of a concerto was to be supplied, the capable pianist was available with eloquent support for Faelten or Strasny.[15]

Under these men Arthur mastered the principles of Classic style and was encouraged in his natural inclination to write music that was primarily expressive in its character and purpose. Formal instruction, however, was not the predominant component of his musical education. He said he derived greater insight from the many opportunities for performance, ensemble work, accompanying, sightreading, and concert-going that were available at the conservatory than from the classwork that was required of him.

> But, bear in mind that the romantic wave was at its crest, 1880–1900, and carried me along with the tide . . . I was fairly caught between the Wagner-Brahms factions, but with an omnivorous appetite, I devoured everything I could lay hands on. Everything was grist to my mill.[16]

It may be in these early experiences that his convictions about the importance of analysis, a conspicuous feature of his teaching in later years, had their beginnings. He felt extended practice in analysis had been lacking in the conservatory classes, and he filled this need himself over the years. His lifelong analysis of the music of the Classic and Romantic masters furnished the mature Shepherd with an understanding of musical devices and constructions which, assimilated into his own style and for his own purposes, enabled him to compose music at once expressive, rich in sonority, skillfully manipulated with regard to its thematic content, and clear in form.

It was a fruitful relationship between Arthur and his teachers: guidance, advice, and experience on the one hand, and on the other an exceptional talent—eager and willing, yet careful to test each tenet for its utility to him, he grafted the expressive urge of an individual musical personality onto an essentially traditional mode of expression. His teachers detected a restless spirit in his music, and they sometimes took exception to his use of dissonance. Yet the musical logic was always so compelling that by 1934 even Goetschius had acknowledged his acceptance of all in Shepherd's music to which he had previously objected.

In 1897, at the age of seventeen, Arthur, president of his class, graduated from the conservatory with honors. Five years in Boston, preceded by five in Idaho, constituted his formal education and the foundation upon which his keen intelligence, his love for reading, and his insatiable curiosity would shape a magnificently cultured and creative life.

SALT LAKE CITY: 1897–1909

Following his graduation Arthur Shepherd returned to Boston with the intention of spending a postgraduate year in composition under Goetschius. Unexpectedly, however, George D. Pyper, manager of the Salt Lake Theater, offered him a position in charge of music for the theater's productions. In 1898, therefore, he returned to Salt Lake City where he rejoined his family, who had by then moved from Paris.

The Salt Lake Theater had been built in 1861–62 at the instigation of Brigham Young to provide wholesome amusement and recreation for the people of Salt Lake City. Since the Union Pacific Railroad would not offer service as far west as Salt Lake City for eight more years, the greater part of the materials and labor used in its construction were of local origin. At the time of its completion it was a completely equipped and modern theater and was the largest building yet constructed by the Mormons—80 by 144 feet on the ground floor and 40 feet high to the square of the building, with a hipped roof covered by a dome.[17] To this theater came famous players: Maude Adams, Nance O'Neill, Fred Ward, Richard Mansfield, and E. H. Sothern. It attracted traveling shows and opera companies and was the home of local dramatic and opera groups and certain sporting events. The theater orchestra, which Shepherd conducted for about six years, varied in size from ten to fifteen players.

Shepherd was also industrious in other pursuits. He reactivated and for four or five years conducted the Salt Lake Symphony Orchestra, presenting one or two concerts each year. He maintained a studio for private teaching and about 1904 was offering classes in harmony and counterpoint. He was also busy as a pianist and accompanist, and occasionally he played for various Salt Lake City churches. He particularly enjoyed his association with Willard Weihe, a talented violinist of Norwegian heritage, with whom he explored the important literature for violin and piano, and on occasion accompanied in public performances. Shepherd was also occupied with studies and composition. He mailed exercises in counterpoint and scoring to Goetschius, for whose "lessons" he paid, so far as the records show, twenty-six dollars between March 2 and October 8 of 1902. One of Goetschius's letters, written in January 1905, bestows general approval on two movements for string quartet but criticizes their texture. Closing on a characteristic note of encouragement, Goetschius calls Shepherd a "great writer," advising him to keep on composing and to publish right away.

In 1901 Shepherd married Hattie Hooper Jennings, a beautiful young woman of one of the older established families of Salt Lake City. Four children were born to them: William Jennings, who died at the age of three; Arthur Phipp; Mary Ann; and Richard Jennings. (This marriage ended in divorce about 1919; the boys were awarded to their father and Ann to her mother. In 1922 Arthur married Grazella Puliver, whom he met in Cleveland through their common interest in music. Born in Kansas, she was at that time an educational representative of the Victor Talking Machine Company. Their son Peter was born in 1930.)

During the years in Salt Lake City, evidence in support of Goetschius's praise accumulated rapidly. Shepherd's catalogue dates the *Overture Joyeuse* for orchestra from 1901. In December 1905 it won the Paderewski Prize of $500.00 and subsequently was performed by both the New York Symphony under Walter Damrosch and the Russian Symphony under Modest Altschuler. About 1905 the Wa-Wan

Salt Lake Theater Orchestra, about 1898. Arthur Shepherd is second from left in back row.

Press published three of his works for piano, and Ditson brought out an anthem in 1907. There are several references in the correspondence to a string quartet, and it is probable that the *Sonata for the Pianoforte,* Op. 4, was written in 1907. This work won first prize in the 1909 contest of the National Federation of Music Clubs and was published in 1911 by the Boston Music Company.

In 1905 Shepherd attended Damrosch's rehearsals and performance of the *Overture Joyeuse* in New York. There he met Lawrence Gilman, the brilliant music critic of *Harper's Weekly,* and Arthur Farwell, idealist, composer, and founder of the Wa-Wan Press. Among these three a discussion of the plight of American composers was inevitable. As Shepherd later wrote to William S. Newman:

> Eventually some of us were reminded that America might find its voice. Chadwick had thought about it; MacDowell in a picture-postcard sort of way, but it wasn't until I met up with Arthur Farwell and Henry Gilbert that my outlook and feeling received a new impulse. My 1st Piano Sonata (last movement) was created in that milieu. Gilbert always ticketed me as an "academic." Well I did know my classics better than "Hank" and wasn't so deeply mired in Wagner as was my old friend Farwell. Those of your own generation can hardly realize the *cross-currents* that beset us fellows at the turn of the century.[18]

An association, a project especially dear to Farwell, was envisioned. About this time, in fact, together with Henry F. Gilbert, he founded the American Music Society, the object of which was "to advance the study and performance of the works of American Composers and the study of all folk-music touching American musical development."[19] The society was composed of members in and about Boston; its headquarters were at Farwell's home in Newton Center, where discussions and recitals of American music were periodically held.

Arthur Farwell (1872–1952) was a man of rich mental endowment and genuine musical talent. Through his mother he was a distant relative of

Ralph Waldo Emerson, which may account for his idealistic turn of mind colored with transcendentalism and mysticism. He had studied in Germany with Humperdinck, at which time he became an enthusiastic Wagnerian. Later, however, he grew to distrust systematic and academic theory and was attracted by the indigenous folk music of America: Indian, Negro, and cowboy tunes. He was obsessed by the idea that American composers should assert their heritage by drawing upon this native material. To drift unconcernedly on a tide of European traditions was, for him, anathema. Thus, though he had discarded Wagnerian technique, the impulse behind it lingered in his attempts to develop forms of expression as closely identified with the American scene as Wagner's were with German culture. This had led him as early as 1901 to create the Wa-Wan Press, through which he published music composed by Americans without regard for its commercial potential. (The name Wa-Wan itself reflected Farwell's nationalistic stand; it referred to an important Omaha Indian ceremony of peace, fellowship, and song.) Though the press concerned itself mostly with composers who were not so thoroughly committed to the European style as was the Boston group—then prominent in American music—it did not limit itself entirely to "nationalistic" music. Shepherd considered Gilbert's *Comedy Overture* the best of its orchestral works, but conceded that no really important instrumental music appeared in the catalog.[20]

In order to spread the influence of the American Music Society, Farwell and Gilbert wrote articles for newspapers and magazines and organized regional chapters, called Wa-Wan Centers, in other cities. Farwell traveled about giving lecture-recitals and enlisting the aid of persons sufficiently interested to carry on a Wa-Wan program once it had been organized. In areas too distant to proselytize personally, he relied on others. Frederic Ayres organized a center in Colorado Springs and Shepherd had one underway in Salt Lake City. At least once Farwell was able to visit the Salt Lake center, but Shepherd was the mainspring of Wa-Wan activity in that area.

There remain about twenty-five of Farwell's letters to Shepherd from the period of 1905 to 1908, during which Shepherd's involvement with the Wa-Wan movement was at its height. Many concern the technical details of the editing and publishing by the press of some of Shepherd's music. The two men discussed and criticized their music, argued over the powers and purposes of music, and in general developed and sharpened their artistic principles through fruitful correspondence.[21] In this way Shepherd was able to keep in touch with musical developments in Boston; this was important to him, for in spite of his accomplishments in Salt Lake City he could not avoid fretting over the inevitable amateurism that pervaded and surrounded his efforts there. It was evident not only in the imperfect performances of his largely volunteer symphony orchestra, but in the lack of critical judgment and appreciation on the part of his audiences and critics. Various communications to friends in Boston indicate his yearning for the more professional musical climate of the East. As early as 1901 a letter from Goetschius, now in the Shepherd Collection, approved his tentative plans for a return to Boston for further study. In 1907 Shepherd wrote of this possibility to Farwell, who, imbued with an almost fanatical zeal for the Wa-Wan Society and needing help with it, encouraged him to make the break.[22] Negotiations continued for some time, and finally Farwell's appeal was successful. Sometime in the latter part of 1908 or early in 1909 Shepherd moved to Newton Center,[23] leaving his family in Salt Lake City.

Shepherd's subsequent relation to the Wa-Wan movement gradually came into conflict with his musical convictions. In Salt Lake City he had been strongly attracted to Farwell and Gilbert and their idealistic venture. He realized that theirs was the only current, organized force devoted to the liberation of the American composer and his music from the domination of European culture. Though Americans had won prestige in literature, business, industry, and science, there was still a preference for European or European-trained musicians over local artists.

> Even today a symphony orchestra with any other than the usual alignment in its personnel—of a foreign conductor, French and Belgian woodwinds; German, Austrian, Italian and Russian strings; German and Middle-European brass—would probably be looked upon as not quite the real thing. I once knew a rawboned Yankee who took to the oboe, and, with typical New England fortitude, he perservered until he became a proficient performer; but he grew a Vandyke beard and grew to look like a Frenchman.[24]

The leaders of the Wa-Wan Society conceded that American musical beginnings had necessarily to be grafted from European stock. Most settlers of the New World had been too busy clearing a wilderness to be occupied with art music, and the few immigrant groups that sponsored organized musical activities—the Moravians, for example—naturally clung to familiar musical habits. Nor did the Wa-

Wan movement propose to excise established musical masterworks from the repertoires of American performers, but rather demanded a hearing for competent American performers and opportunities for the music of American composers to be played. By the turn of the century the United States looked back over more than a hundred years of autonomous existence. It had developed indigenous political, social, and economic patterns. In Farwell's view the time had come for American music to be heard in an American dialect:

> Of fundamental importance is it to recognize that now is the moment of breaking away from that in the past which is thwarting to present growth, from the special styles and forms of music that have expressed the individuality of other lands to forms that shall express the individuality of our own. Undoubtedly the magnitude, the largeness of spirit, the seriousness of the great works of the past are to be retained, but not their outgrown meaning for the race, nor their outgrown technical system. It will no longer be a virtue that an American musical work shall tally the outlines and colors of the works of the German or of the Russian or French masters. We have passed the Imitative stage and have entered upon the Creative, when our musical works must stand by the possession of qualities not shared by works of any other time or place. For, failing this, individuality fails, and failing individuality we can have no significant nor dynamic musical art. For it is the establishment of an appropriate and vitalized individuality that insures universal significance in any art. Excellence in imitation, however great, cannot lead us out of the Egypt of lifeless provincialism into the promised land of creative art.[25]

With much of this Shepherd could agree. He had already given more than moral support through his work in the establishment and guidance of the Wa-Wan Center in Salt Lake City. Though his primary objective in returning to the East was further study with Goetschius, he also intended to assist with the program that Farwell had outlined in the letter quoted above. Years later Shepherd still spoke out in support of the Wa-Wan's mission:

> All in all the independent spirit of such men as Arthur Farwell, Henry Gilbert, Harvey Worthington Loomis, did register effectively, and the name of Lawrence Gilman must not be forgotten in this connection, for he too saw the significance of this movement, and contributed effective propaganda in the columns of Harper's Weekly. . . . I am glad to have been a participant and have done my bit along the lines so enthusiastically sponsored by Arthur Farwell, whose talent and idealism are not fully appreciated.[26]

On the other hand, Shepherd could not see eye-to-eye with the Wa-Wan strategy. Farwell and Gilbert demanded both of the composer and audience a conscious preference for American folk music:

> Every corner of America today has its appropriate musical expression, and it matters little whether that expression be in a primitive or in a more highly developed condition. It is enough that these forces are alive, growing and characteristic. If we will live the whole musical life of our country, sympathizing with and enjoying its every aspect, rougher and more refined, wherever beauty and truth of expression are found, we must realize that a musical democratization of our natures alone will enable us to do so. There must be a willingness on our part to be, in our imaginations or our sympathies, at a moment's notice, a cowboy ranging the plains, a Southern planter taking his leisure or his slave at work, an Omaha chief watching the approach of the Thunder god; or with equal readiness we are to share the idealizations of these motives through the tonal medium of our more immediate fellow man, the composer—or still other motives, nameless, innumerable, expressible only in tone, revealing the peculiar sense of beauty or of spiritual aspiration of our time.[27]

By way of example, Farwell and Gilbert used these native materials. Moreover, in their desire to avoid European influences they shunned many of the traditional devices, forms, and methods of composition. They isolated themselves from the established American composers, particularly those connected with the New England Conservatory and the universities of the region. Their chauvinism forced them to brand the works of the Boston School as academic and unrepresentative of their time and place.

Perhaps they were right. The music of George W. Chadwick, Arthur Foote, Horatio Parker, and other prominent composers of that time is not today a vital force in American music. On the other hand, neither is Farwell's nor Gilbert's. Though full of zeal and in some ways fresh and new when it appeared, their art now has an air of quaintness. In Shepherd's opinion neither brought a really commanding technique to his work. Consequently they could neither express nor fully realize their otherwise admirable ideals.[28]

For his part, Shepherd could not renounce European technique and the whole historic tradition of Western music—of which, in his estimation, American music is merely an extension. Blessed with musical ingenuity, he used it wherever it suited his purpose. He saw no reason to abandon age-old devices—"stunts" in Farwell's idiom—merely because they had not been invented by Americans. He agreed that American music should express an American spirit, but he believed that this expression would arise naturally in the work of an American genius imbued with the ethos of his heritage and working his way through to its realization in a personal musical utterance, without conscious *a priori* use or rejection of specific materials and methods.

Thus, unable to give himself wholeheartedly to the Wa-Wan cause, Shepherd cast about for other endeavors. The opportunity to teach at his alma mater opened up; and in 1910, assured of a measure of permanence, he established his home in Boston and brought his wife and three children from Salt Lake City to be with him.[29]

THE TRIUMPH OF TRADITION: 1909–1920

Finally, about 1909 (I think) I decided upon a more definite program, & took up residence in Boston; lived for a while in the home of A. Farwell in Newton Center and applied for a teaching position at N. E. Conservatory. Chadwick, under whom I studied during my graduating year, was very friendly & took me aboard. I was assigned to teach harmony. The breaking-in period was not easy. Eventually, following the death of Benj. Cutter I was given his place in the department. Cutter was a marvellous teacher, and put me on the trail of sound pedagogical procedures in analysis (in particular) and fostered my enthusiasm for exploration. Feeling at times overburdened with heavy class routine, I re-arranged my schedule to include piano instruction.[30]

Had Arthur Shepherd been longing for this? Had the example of Percy Goetschius, the indefatigable student and teacher, lurked in his memory during the decade in Salt Lake City? The Wa-Wan episode had been an adventure, an exhilarating flirt with a radical cause. It had excited him, impelled him to activity, and kept his mind on the outer world. The Wa-Wan Press had published some of his music—piano pieces and songs—but as Charles Martin Loeffler once pointed out, these works did not embody the Wa-Wan spirit nearly so well as, say, Farwell's *Pawnee Horses.* Shepherd's works never struck hard for the cause; they were mainstream compositions. They were probably published through friendship and out of gratitude for creating the Wa-Wan Center in Salt Lake City, for it seems more than coincidence that the Press brought out nothing of his after the *Five Songs,* Op. 7, in 1909, the year that he joined the conservatory faculty. Thereafter he published through the established commercial houses.

The break with Farwell represented the triumph of tradition in Arthur Shepherd's artistic life. It marked the end of a period of conscious nationalism that had begun about 1905 at his meeting with Farwell and Gilman in New York. He never lost his sympathy for the Wa-Wan movement and all that it represented, or his regard for Farwell and Gilbert, and in later years he championed American music on every occasion; but he had been too heavily influenced, possibly not so much by Goetschius himself as by the beauty of the music that was the basis of the conservatory course. When he had to make a choice, Shepherd chose tradition. The choice was prophetic. In his conservatism lay Shepherd's weakness as well as his strength.

At the conservatory he taught harmony classes, gave piano lessons, played chamber music, and conducted the school orchestra whenever Chadwick or Wallace Goodrich relinquished the baton.[31] He adapted quickly. As early as 1910 he had gained sufficient professional standing to address a convention of the Music Teachers National Association on the subject of harmony teaching.[32]

Benjamin Cutter died on May 10, 1910. This former teacher and admired colleague had set an unforgettable example, and the list of his qualities and attributes as a teacher is generally descriptive of Shepherd also. Cutter possessed a keen analytic mind and the eloquence for vivid communication with his students. He was intensely curious about the newest music as well as the masterworks of the past. He based his teaching upon convictions derived from personal analysis as well as from analytic literature. Cutter wrote his own harmony text; this Shepherd did nòt do, but he always esteemed this work of Cutter's. Indeed, at one time Shepherd seriously considered the addition of new musical examples to Cutter's *Harmonic Analysis* to bring it up to date for republication.

Certain scholarly interests appealed to Shepherd at this time, but they never developed into solid musicological endeavors; perhaps he lacked the patience for extended research. Shepherd's predilection lay in the practical value of music for his students and in his own particular needs as a composer and performer. When he did take up the pen, he wrote well; and over a long life he produced a number of articles, lectures, program notes, critiques, and at least one book. His natural mode of communication was, however, the spoken rather than the written word, as is attested by a host of former students and colleagues.

The New England Conservatory and the Ivy League universities were repositories of musical traditionalism in America at the turn of the century. They were staffed by Amerian composers who had studied in Europe, a tradition begun in 1862 when John Knowles Paine, returning from Berlin, offered a class at Harvard. Horatio Parker became a professor at Yale in 1894, Edward MacDowell joined Columbia's faculty in 1896, and George W. Chadwick was appointed director of the New England Conservatory in 1897, the year of Shepherd's graduation. Shepherd's opinions of these men survive in various lectures and articles of his late Cleveland period. He recognized the value of some of their work: "They bear the marks, to be sure, of the European conservatory, but they reveal, nevertheless heartening indications of individual artistic virility."[33]

For the most part, however, their music struck him as but pale reflections of the divergent movements that fragmented musical Romanticism in the last quarter of the nineteenth century. He admired their energy, their ideals, and their devotion to their art. For Chadwick's music he could even feel some enthusiasm. He detected in it a certain jaunty American spirit that appealed to him and that he considered more genuinely indigenous than MacDowell's stylized Americanisms. But most of the music of these men seemed to Shepherd only a generation removed from the choirloft. He considered it uniformly infected by the Romantic "blight of the appoggiatura." He attributed its eventual debility to the mildness of its utterance. In spite of an occasional dalliance with American themes (especially in MacDowell), it was lacking in evangelical fervor. "They worked and contributed as musicians of integrity and talent—each in his own manner,"[34] but as a group they did not make a serious attempt to imbue their art with an indigenous American spirit.

For Charles Martin Loeffler and Charles Tomlinson Griffes, however, Shepherd had profound respect.

> To return to my Boston period, I recall the somewhat snobbish attitude of various musicians and "big-wigs" of the established order, and there were, of course, many lively discussions on the side concerning the artistic merit of the Wa-Wan output. One composer, however, of unquestioned eminence was openminded and very cordial to the new spirit manifested in this venture. I refer to Charles Martin Loeffler, whose genius and culture was always an incentive, and many of us owe to him more than can actually be put down in words.[35]
>
> You mention Loeffler, oh yes, he was an influence by reason of a most impressive culture; critical acumen taste and artistic integrity unmatched by his immediate Boston Contemporaries. He too saw the urgent need for us fellows to emancipate ourselves from the incubus of German romanticism. I remember his expressing regret that he had not been born in America! I have in my possession a set of wild-west stories by Clarence Mulford ("Hopalong Cassidy" etc.) presented to me by Loeffler. What a paradox from a musician who was once almost like a family member in the home of G. Fauré.
>
> Yes I recall passages from L's works of great beauty; such as the long beautiful cello solo in the coda of "By the Waters of Babylon." . . . He *was* a melodist of true distinction.[36]

Among other activities in prewar Boston, Shepherd conducted the Musical Art Society, a women's chorus. But in 1917, after three seasons, he found it necessary to resign in protest of the refusal of certain of the society's officers to permit a performance of Loeffler's *Psalm 137, By the Rivers of Babylon.*[37]

Loeffler encouraged Farwell and Gilbert in their use of folk songs, and occasionally his own music was influenced by jazz. He had a deep and sincere interest in American culture and its literature (particularly the West), but on the whole it was so essentially foreign to his own temperament and background that he could not successfully use indigenous American materials in his own work. In a similarly encouraging vein Loeffler once asked Shepherd why he had not written a violin sonata, an offhand question that apparently led to the composition of the *Sonata pour violon et piano* (c. 1916–1920).[38] Shepherd related that "the best lesson I ever had" occurred when he took the new sonata to Loeffler and together they spent two or three hours reading through and discussing it.

Of Charles Tomlinson Griffes it is also best to let Shepherd speak for himself:

> Griffes studied with Humperdinck but turned out to be one of our most distinguished eclectics. He was extraordinarily sensitive to the impressionistic trend. I heard him state once that he knew his Debussy and Ravel from beginning to end, and none would have been quicker to acknowledge their influence than he. But he was just as sensitively aware of later trends and had within himself the power to explore and assimilate to an extraordinary degree. I look upon the point at which he changed his style, as one of the most significant manifestations in our American music; not hinging altogether upon the precise merits of the works themselves (which are indeed of a high order) but because of the truly creative, modern sensibility revealed therein. . . .[39]

Despite a heavy teaching load Shepherd managed to compose, and gradually his music won increasing recognition. In addition to the early publications and prizes already mentioned, he won another prize in the 1909 contest of the National Federation of Music Clubs for his song *The Lost Child.* In 1913 he again won the National Federation of Music Clubs prize with the cantata, *The City in the Sea,* on a poem by Bliss Carman. Other works completed prior to his enlistment in 1918 were *Overture, The Festival of Youth* (1915); *Fantasy for Piano and Orchestra* (1916); *The Nuptials of Attila* for orchestra, date unknown; and a number of small choral pieces. Performances of these works were given in Chicago, St. Louis, New York, and Boston and helped greatly to spread his influence in the musical circles of the northeastern section of the country.

On July 3, 1918, Arthur Shepherd enlisted in the United States Army as a bandleader at Camp Devens, Massachusetts, and was assigned to Headquarters Company of the 303rd Field Artillery. Within two weeks, on July 16, he sailed for France where he served nearly eight months, arriving back home on March 12, 1919. He had no unauthorized absences and is credited with participation in the battles of the Toul Sector, November 4–10, 1918. His honorary discharge gives his description at the time of his induction: "38 6/12 years, brown hair, brown eyes, fair complexion, 5′ 6½″." For several months his band was stationed in the village of Aubiére in the Puy-de-Dôme region of France near Clermont-Ferrand and Vichy, where he lived with a peasant family. Life was primitive; most of the inhabitants enjoyed neither electricity nor other conveniences. His men ridiculed the country and its people, irritating Shepherd, who had acquired a keen appreciation of French intellect through recent music he had studied in Boston. He could feel a sympathy for these simple rural people that was quite beyond the comprehension of some of his fellows. The band played for the various military functions in the area and visited military hospitals and rest areas to entertain the soldiers. While "sitting around" in France, Shepherd wrote marches; one of these, *Marche Solonelle,* he later revised for orchestra.

Commenting on his return to America, Shepherd wrote:

> Following the war, I faced very serious domestic problems. There was much unrest and a general "letdown" in Boston music life. There was something of an exodus including a breaking of ranks in the Boston Symphony orchestra. N. Sokoloff (formerly a B. Symph. member) turned up in Boston in search of an assistant conductor [for Cleveland]. He consulted Carl Engel who in turn recommended me for the position. So I bade good bye to Boston and came on to Cleveland.[40]

Actually Shepherd had resumed his prewar activities of composing and teaching at the conservatory. The *Overture to a Drama* was written then, though not performed until 1924.[41] The domestic crisis he referred to eventually ended in divorce, and it may have been that the desire for a change of scene enhanced the attractiveness of Sokoloff's offer. Nikolai Sokoloff was conductor of the newly formed orchestra in Cleveland, where many kinds of cultural undertakings were being considered. One of his letters states that he had recommended Shepherd to the "Directors" as head of the "Conservatory project," and had offered him the post of assistant conductor of the Cleveland Orchestra.[42] Shepherd accepted the orchestral position, and in 1920 he moved to Cleveland, where he was to spend the remainder of his life.

Author's Note: At this point readers who are especially interested in the music may find it worthwhile to turn to Chapter 7, in which Shepherd's early compositions are discussed in greater detail.

CLEVELAND

CHAPTER 2

In 1952 Shepherd wrote of Cleveland: "This large industrial and manufacturing center, for the past hundred years, has shown consistent and expansive development in the fine arts, with music and drama in the foreground. Few cities west of the Atlantic seaboard, in fact, can claim a richer or more abundant cultural life."[1] Organized musical activity had begun there in the late 1830s, largely as a result of the arrival of music-loving immigrants from Central Europe. By the middle of the nineteenth century musical events were a normal part of the city's life and were presented both by local talent and by traveling artists, groups, and orchestras. In 1899 the Metropolitan Opera Company presented its first season in Cleveland, and it has had strong support ever since. The Cleveland Orchestra was organized in 1918 and rather quickly achieved a place among the better orchestras of the United States.

The Cleveland of 1920, when Arthur Shepherd arrived, was a city in which large fortunes had been and were still being accumulated. Indicative of this wealth were the mansions that sprang up by the hundreds, each on carefully groomed and ample grounds. In summer these became as isolated little kingdoms, each hedged or walled and covered almost solidly overhead with the dense foliage of the elms, sycamores, and other trees for which Cleveland is known as "The Forest City." The wealthy inhabitants of these mansions had a high regard for the accoutrements of culture. Institutions such as Western Reserve University, the Cleveland Museum of Art, the Cleveland Orchestra, the Western Reserve Historical Society, and the Cleveland Museum of Natural History enjoyed generous financial support and energetic management.

Who were the patrons of these considerable cultural endeavors, and how do they bear on Arthur Shepherd's story? The best answers that I can offer come from a vivid communication—a tape-recorded letter—sent to me in 1967 by Grazella P. Shepherd, the composer's second wife. Here and later I shall quote extensively from this fascinating letter, revising her words only where the necessities of formal writing supersede the informality of what is essentially one side of a conversation.

> You asked about our friends—what kind of a world Arthur Shepherd lived in. Arturus and I were married in May 1922. In June that year Dudley Blossom came to our little house—our little apartment really, it was, on Hessler Road: you know, just a little street close to the university where we lived—and drove us out to Harrywold, which was the home of the Binghams (Mrs. Blossom's family) in Bratenahl. It was a beautiful house, a big, old, roomy house; high, with a marvelous fireplace in a room ideal for the making of music. This evening came about because Dud was deeply concerned with the orchestra to which Arturus had come as assistant conductor, where he was associated with Nikolai Sokoloff as conductor, and of course Adella Prentiss Hughes, the manager. Dud liked to play the violin and it was to play sonatas that . . . we were asked to go there. I remember they played, I think, Grieg and César Franck, and we had a beautiful, beautiful time, the four of us. That friendship has lasted through the years. The men are gone but Betty—Mrs. Elizabeth Blossom—and I are still the dearest of friends. In a way this shows the world in which we were to live. Through the Blossoms, and through the whole set of the orchestra, we came to be very, I would say, intimate friends with Mr. and Mrs. Brewster (Mr. Brewster was also connected with the administration of that new orchestra), with Grover Higgins, and with Frank Ginn and his wife. . . .

And I'd like to speak of Florence Brewster and her husband, because through them many, many things happened without names attached. I really think that Severance Hall[2] came about as it did, when it did, because of the—shall I say—insistence of Florence Brewster. The Brewsters talked constantly with Betty and Dud; Dud talked with Mr. Ginn; Mr. Ginn with Mr. Severance. Florence had extraordinary perception of need, and she knew how to find the people to meet the need. She had the courage and the grace to do it well.

Mr. Ginn was, I suppose one might say, really an artist, only he very early knew that he must make a living. . . . He became a lawyer, one of the truly great lawyers of Cleveland, but he never gave up his interest in the arts. Mr. and Mrs. Ginn had owned a summer house in Gates Mills, a lovely suburb of Cleveland. They built onto that house a great music room, and a gallery and green house. The music room was hung with Monets and Manets and Degas, and supplied with a library of chamber music. There Arthur Shepherd played constantly with violinists or chamber music groups. There [Josef] Fuchs, the Cleveland Quartet, [and] Carlton Cooley, among others, supplied program after program while Mrs. Ginn served beautiful food and Frank beautiful wine.

Grover Higgins was a member of the Ginn firm. [He] was passionately fond of chamber music, particularly quartets. And he frequently gave concerts in his own home played by the Budapest Quartet, the Flonzaley [Quartet] and the Cleveland String Quartet; and Joe Fuchs, Carlton Cooley, people of this nature. Grover Higgins left an endowment for chamber music which has created the permanent structure of the Cleveland Chamber Music Society, now thoroughly established in Cleveland. In the days that this all began it was almost impossible to get a hundred people into the Chamber Music Hall of Severance [Hall] for a chamber music concert. Now they are sold out. Some of it, at least, goes back to Grover's gift, which stabilized the whole. Incidentally, Grover paid for the publication of several pieces of Arturus's. Grover went to Boston, as did Mrs. Blossom and Mrs. Brewster, for the performance of Arturus's Second Symphony there.[3]

Shepherd's duties with the Cleveland Orchestra required him to play the piano, conduct the chorus, rehearse or conduct the orchestra, write the program notes, and give preconcert lectures on the music to be played. Children's concerts, conducted by Nikolai Sokoloff, were initiated in collaboration with the Cleveland Public Schools in the season of 1921–22. The next season Shepherd conducted about half of these, and beginning in 1924 he conducted all of them. He was responsible for the selection of music, for the instruction of the children at the concert, and—with Alice Keith, Supervisor of Music Appreciation in the Cleveland Public Schools—for the formulation of pedagogic objectives and methods. Together they instituted a Music Memory Contest for the children, for which they wrote a booklet discussing the music performed at the concerts, *Listening In on the Masters.*

The concerts were heavily attended, with audiences of as many as 2,300 pupils at a performance. They were played not only in Masonic Hall, the orchestra's home in the early years, but at certain high schools and in other cities when the orchestra was on tour. Shepherd prepared concerts on the evolution of the orchestra, nature in music, the symphony, and the music of several countries. From press reviews one gains the impression of a businesslike, rather brisk conductor who had an easygoing way with the children. He explained the music, demonstrated the instruments, asked and answered questions. Undertaking this work with enthusiasm, he was particularly sensitive to the challenge of choosing appropriate music for the children. "In trying to gauge the receptive powers of children, one may easily make mistakes. One is just as likely to under-rate than [*sic*] to over-rate their powers. It is not always the loud or the fast piece that has the greatest appeal."[4]

The program notes that Shepherd furnished for the third through twelfth orchestra seasons, 1920–30, were written for average concertgoers. He included stories and anecdotes about the composers and music and frequently quoted letters to orient his readers to the philosophic and aesthetic concepts under which the music was created. Musical analyses usually consisted of a more or less chronological description of those features of a score that could be recognized by an average listener. Program music and opera excerpts required a synopsis of the story; songs were often handled merely by printing the text. Occasionally, however, Shepherd indulged in observations of a more technical nature, as, for instance, his description of the retransition in the first movement of Beethoven's *Eroica* Symphony:

> The recapitulation section is reached through the highly original procedure of unrelated harmonies, the principal theme being announced mysteriously in the tonic of the original key against which there is a string tremolo on the dominant seventh of the same tonality. This passage must be put down as a stroke of genius, inasmuch as it anticipates one of the most interesting and characteristic procedures—known as polyharmony—of present day composers.[5]

Sometimes he shared more personal and reflective views about the music:

> It is now one hundred years, lacking thirty days, since the premiere of Beethoven's Ninth Symphony and the many anniversary performances throughout the world bear testimony to the undisputed sway of the supreme genius, whose great rugged spirit found its most elo-

quent utterance in this his last work for orchestra. There was an interim of eleven years between the eighth and ninth symphonies, the composer's life during this period was agitated and beset with many difficulties, quarrels, distractions, bargainings, family perplexities and law suits to which were added the manifold troubles incurred through the guardianship of his nephew Karl. An entry in his diary dating from the early part of 1818, indicates the composer's distressed state of mind. "God, O God, my Guardian, my Rock, my All, Thou seest my heart and knowest how it distresses me to do harm to others through doing right to my darling Karl. Hear Thou unutterable! Hear Thy unhappy, most unhappy of mortals!" Beethoven endured privations and anxieties and his domestic life was attended by squalid disorder. Was all this turmoil the necessary seeding ground for the great symphony which was to crown the succession of orchestral masterpieces?

The might of Beethoven's genius burns ever brighter through the passing ages by reason of his God-given power to transcend the vanities and vexations of life and to give utterance at last to his soul's aspirations in a paean of joy.

Many a second or third rate composer has waxed eloquent on the theme of human woes, but the significant fact remains that it took a Bach, a Handel, a Mozart, and a Beethoven to voice the triumph of hope and joy.[6]

Sokoloff had planned to conduct this first performance of the *Choral* Symphony in Cleveland himself, but he was unable to appear because of illness. Shepherd conducted and has described it as among his greatest musical thrills.[7]

In these days the Shepherds were living in an apartment, and for a description of their life there we turn again to Mrs. Shepherd's account:

We had other friends too. We lived, as I said, on Hessler Road, which was a small street where people that were beginning their lives lived, and there we fell in with a group which afterwards we always spoke of as "Hessler Oads." That group was made up of lawyers, architects, artists. They had less money than the other people of whom I've spoken, but they had great qualities of being which endeared them to us very much. One was "Tony" (Antonio) Dinardo, an Italian architect and painter; and his wife was also an artist. But the thing I think that flashes through our minds when we think of Tony Dinardo was a laugh that came from the very depths of his being, and was so infectious that I have seen whole restaurant groups who didn't know him join in laughter simply because it was such a real laugh. That little group, the "Hessler Oads" nurtured [its] members . . . by the most beautiful understanding. Over the years . . . I have not known in that group gossip. I've never known a time when there wasn't interesting discussion of interesting ideas.

There were the evenings . . . of incessant music. Arturus had a grand piano in a second floor bedroom of our house. In looking back I don't see how we ever got the piano there, but I remember the house bathed in sound. And it was to this house that [Ernst von] Dohnányi, and the Cleveland Quartet, [the composer] Douglas Moore of the Art Museum, Beryl Rubenstein of the Music Institute, [Andre de] Ribaupierre and Ernest Bloch came. . . . [Also] Roger Sessions was one of the people who came to that house. . . .

It was here . . . that Arturus's two sons by a former marriage [Arthur and Richard] came to live with us. It was while we were there, too, that Arturus and I lived in the Blossom house—not the one in Bratenahl but the one built out on Cedar Road—for several summers; and I think it was there that *Horizons* was made.[8]

Shepherd wrote only a few small works during the early years in Cleveland. Goetschius, in a letter dated January 1921, referred to an earlier remark made by Shepherd that his duties were too demanding to permit much composition; still, Goetschius advised him not to look about for a change yet, but rather to demand more leisure.[9] Meanwhile, Shepherd had already received offers for other positions. Dr. C. W. Morrison, director of Oberlin Conservatory, wrote Goetschius, "If Mr. Shepherd does not accept the position open in Oberlin it will be for other reasons than a lack of warm commendation from such authorities as yourself and Mr. George W. Chadwick."[10]

Most impressive was an offer from Goetschius himself, who was retiring and wanted Shepherd to step into his place as head of the Department of Theory and Composition at the Institute of Musical Art in New York City.

And now, lad, I want you to think favorably of this position here at the Institute, as my follower at the *head* of the department of Theory and Composition. It is the finest position of its kind in this country—I believe, in the world. For I know of no musical Academy *anywhere* that measures up to the high standards, seriousness, dignity, and almost perfection of methods, that we possess here. The work is not very exacting. My assistants have all been so thoroughly schooled and trained (excuse me for adding, in my methods of teaching) that every student who comes to you in the higher classes is sure to have been thoroughly prepared. You have simply to "continue" with them. And the whole course (of 7 years) has been so accurately systematized, that you will find the subject of *every lesson* indicated, and will lose no time in arranging the students' work—of course, until you have entered fully into the "machinery" of it, and find it advisable or necessary to make *your own* personal digressions. The Lessons follow my five or six books, closely. You will have little "explaining" to do—it is all given in the indicated paragraphs of the books.—And you will be absolutely free for over four months in the Summer, consecutively, which will surely give you time for your own life work—composition.

And what it may lead to in the future, you may almost forecast. The "leaders" are growing older—someone, young and enthusiastic, must take their place, in time.—

Manchester, N.H.
Dec. 27. 1924.

Dear Arthur:

I am disappointed, deeply disappointed, for I know of no one else, to whom I should be willing to entrust the continuation of my work here.

But I understand your side of the question fully, thanks to your very explicit and open-hearted presentation, and I can only assume that you are exercising wise judgment.

I was glad to learn that your present position is such a congenial one, and so well remunerated. I did not suspect that you were so very well situated, financially, or I might almost have hesitated to mention this position in N.Y. —— I still believe, however, absolutely, that this position in N.Y. would mean more to you in the long run, in permanency and advancement, than what you now have. This position in N.Y. would be for life. ---

Well. I must look further. Do you know of any one?

Forgive me, if this letter seems too short. I know of nothing more to say. Of course you would not reconsider?-?-

With very cordial greetings and best wishes for the New Year from us both, to you and all your dear ones,

Affectionately,
Percy Goetschius

Think it over, and let us know what we may hope for as soon as you can.[11]

Shepherd declined the offer for reasons that Goetschius reviewed in his answer, a facsimile of which appears above.

During 1925 Shepherd prepared articles for *Cobbett's Cyclopedic Survey of Chamber Music* on the following composers: Frederic Ayres, Mrs. H. H. A. Beach, Frederick Shepherd Converse, Carl Engel, Rubin Goldmark, Henry Hadley, William Clifford Heilman, Henry Holden Huss, Daniel Gregory Mason, David Stanley Smith, and Edgar Stillman-Kelley. In his analyses he emphasized good craftsmanship wherever it appeared. He seldom objected to a composer's usage without immediately mentioning some praiseworthy aspect of his work. "There are more finished craftsmen than Ayres, but few among his American contemporaries possessed of equal lyrical intensity."[12] Although in a few cases he revealed his personal preferences, he probably suppressed adverse judgements to the end that each composer might appear in his best light. Shepherd's willingness to see the good, both in music and in its composers, continued throughout his life. But he was not uncritical; he had definite opinions about musical values and aesthetics, and he was not in the least hesitant to defend his estimates of this or that device, technique, or piece. However, his opinions for public dissemination were usually censored in accordance with his belief that criticism is most valuable when constructive, that within such limits much can be implied about the merits of a work. "... A work in every way typical of a composer who is never concerned with profundity, nor with tonal and atonal experiments. Spontaneity, verve and expert craftsmanship are the characteristic features of his work."[13] It is an attitude that shows Shepherd at his best, reveals his genuine desire to help others, and in part explains the good impressions that he made. Douglas Moore once wrote to him: "I can't tell you how much we enjoyed having you here for the Festival. You brought a youthful spirit to our jaded atmosphere. I wish all composers were as open minded and generous to their contemporaries as you ..."[14]

As music editor of the Cleveland *Press* from October 1928 to September 1931, Shepherd gained further experience in criticism. According to Arthur Quimby:

> As a critic he again exhibited a fine catholicity of taste, and an openness of mind. I well remember how he damned Bloch's *America* when he first heard it, and how he willingly reversed all that when a second hearing convinced him of its worth. No false pride, or narrowness of outlook.[15]

In 1926, after the orchestra's eighth season, Shepherd resigned his post as assistant conductor, and at the beginning of the 1927–28 academic year he joined the faculty of Cleveland College of Western Reserve University as a lecturer in music. He continued as conductor of the Children's Concerts, however, until the end of the 1927–28 season.[16] By this move Shepherd gained time for composition. He enjoyed teaching again, and in 1928 he was elevated to the post of Professor of Music in the graduate school of the university.

At about this time the relationship between the Shepherds and the Blossoms ripened into what could be considered an exemplary instance of twentieth-century patronage. It is likely that many of Shepherd's works after 1930 owe their existence to activities and living conditions made possible by the Blossoms' encouragement and support. In Mrs. Shepherd's words:

> I want to back up a little to Dud too—Dudley Blossom—because he and his wife Elizabeth Bingham Blossom played so great a part in the evolution of the [Cleveland] orchestra and in Arthur Shepherd's life. Dud was gay, wonderfully gay; respectful of human personality. He was an artist without a medium, who poured his life into trying to make life a little better for people less fortunate than himself.[17] Among the many lovely things that were created for Arturus was a concert, given in the Blossoms' new house on Cedar Road, of various of his works. . . . This was greatly aided too by Mrs. Hughes's[18] concern, and her help in making the program, and the beautiful printing of it. . . .
>
> Then there came a time in the late twenties when Mr. and Mrs. Blossom asked us if we would like to live on Richmond Road, which was out near their Cedar house. If so they would build a house for us to rent on an acre . . . of old apple trees. This came about. The place was named "Apple Acre."[19]

Mrs. Shepherd speaks of their life in this house. "Houses have great influence on people," and this one greatly affected them. She mentions that the orchard isolated it from the nearby houses, that the garden had been planted with hundreds of bulbs, that the house was open both to sun and air. She describes carrying Peter, their newborn son, to the house in a clothesbasket and explains that, at this time, Shepherd's older sons were away at school: Arthur at Ohio State and Richard at Harvard.

> . . . the wonderful openness of it. I'm sure there were dark days, and I'm sure there were cold days. I know there was endless snow, and I know we got stuck in the car many times. But still my memory of that place is of a sun-flooded place in bloom; and suffused with music. . . . Arturus had a little music room at one end of the house, and he played whenever he was home. Again, I'm sure he played many other things, but the things I best remember are Bach—always Bach—Schumann, Schubert. But Debussy [and] Fauré [also] seem to me to fit that house.[20]

At this time Shepherd was still music critic for the Cleveland *Press.* After concerts he wrote his reviews at the newspaper offices in downtown Cleveland. By the time he arrived at the house, which was well out from the center of town—almost in the country, in fact—it would be one or two o'clock in the morning. At nine he was due in his office at the university. Mrs. Shepherd worked at Cleveland College of the university as well as serving part of the time as chairman of the Women's Committee of the Cleveland Orchestra. "I don't know how there was energy to do the things we did," she states. But the Shepherds believed and practiced the theory that "we'll never get far with education until we make it more social. . . . The stream of life through that place was constant": Severin Eisenberger, pianist; Arthur Farwell, composer; "Hon" [Mahonri] Young, sculptor, grandson of Brigham Young and long an intimate of Arthur Shepherd; his brothers Albert, Charles, and Harry Shepherd.

> Among the people who came to the house were . . . Arthur Loesser, who played Arturus's music—still does—and was a highly sympathetic and interesting friend, . . . Marie Kraft, a singer memorable because of her art and her faithful projection of the composer's intent. Harold Miles, Herbert Elwell, and Arthur Shepherd are equally indebted to Marie Kraft. . . . [Also] the members of the Walden String Quartet, which was greatly aided in its beginning years by the counsel and friendship of both Arthur Quimby and Arthur Shepherd. . . . Alvin Etler [and James] Aliferis were also part of life. Jimmy Aliferis was a choral conductor, excellent musician, devoted to Arturus. And Alvin Etler was a composer of promise. The hours and hours that went into the kind of companionship to nurture a composer were freely, freely given. . . . I very often think that he [Shepherd] was, for a few of these people, what Max Perkins was in the publishing world, and which he himself never had from another. This was one of the great, great lacks and he always realized it. The nearest he came to this, as I knew him, was during the time of the intimacies with Beryl Rubinstein and Herbert Elwell. Beryl in particular spent as many hours in the consideration of the musical problems of Arthur Shepherd's work as Arthur Shepherd did spend on Beryl's work. It was a particular and peculiar loss to Arturus when Beryl died.[21]

In 1929 Shepherd and Grazella traveled to England, Scotland, and the Continent. They visited relatives, saw the sights of London, and attended the concerts at Covent Garden. They journeyed to Lausanne, where Shepherd performed his *Sonata for Pianoforte and Violin* with André de Ribaupierre

FRANCES NEWSOM, SOPRANO

MARIE SIMMELINK, MEZZO-CONTRALTO

ARTHUR SHEPHERD, PIANO

AND

THE CLEVELAND STRING QUARTET

ARTHUR BECKWITH, FIRST VIOLIN
RALPH SILVERMAN, SECOND VIOLIN
CARLTON COOLEY, VIOLA
VICTOR DE GOMEZ, VIOLONCELLO

WEDNESDAY EVENING, APRIL 21, 1926

AT THE RESIDENCE OF MR. AND MRS. D. S. BLOSSOM

RICHMOND ROAD, SOUTH EUCLID, OHIO

Program

COMPOSITIONS BY ARTHUR SHEPHERD

Allegro con brio
Andante placido
Scherzo Allegro ironico
From String Quartet in G minor

Songs with pianoforte accompaniment:
Nocturne
"There is a light in thy blue eyes"
The lost child
Rhapsody
Poems by James Russell Lowell

Scherzo, giocoso e secco
Andante, con moto
Allegro agitato
From Sonata for pianoforte and violin in G minor

Three Songs for soprano and string quartet:
"He it is"
"The day is no more"
"Light, my Light"
Poems from "Gitanjali," by Rabindranath Tagore

Compositions by Arthur Shepherd

* Theme and Variations for Pianoforte, opus 1.
* Mazurka } opus 2
* Prelude }
* Sonata, F minor, for pianoforte, opus 4.
Fantasy for pianoforte and orchestra.
Prelude and Fugue, E minor, for pianoforte.
Sonata for pianoforte.
Fugue, C sharp minor, for pianoforte.
From a Mountain Lake, for pianoforte.

Songs
* Five Songs, opus 7. Poems by Lowell.
* The Gentle Lady.
* The Lost Child.
* A Star in the night.
"Oh like a Queen.
* "The Lord hath brought again Zion," for baritone solo, chorus and orchestra.
* "The City in the Sea," for chorus of mixed voices and orchestra. Poem by Bliss Carman.
Two choruses for Women's Voices:
Song of the Sea Wind.
"He came all so still."

Anthems
* "O Jesu who art gone before?"
* "Deck thyself, my soul" (response).

Chamber Music
Sonata, G minor, for pianoforte and violin.
String Quartet, G minor.
Three Songs for high voice and string quartet
Poems by Tagore.
Dedicated to Adella Prentiss Hughes.

* Published

Compositions—continued

Orchestra
Overture, "Joyeuse."
Overture, "The Festival of Youth."
Overture, "The Nuptials of Attila."
* Overture to a Drama.
Dedicated to Nikolai Sokoloff.

Performances

Overture Joyeuse, by Russian Symphony Orchestra, under Altschuler, in New York, in 1903; by the New York Symphony Society, under Damrosch, in Salt Lake City, in 1905.

Sonata, opus 4, at Annual Convention of National Federation of Music Clubs, Grand Rapids, Michigan, in 1909.

The Lost Child, at Annual Convention of National Federation of Music Clubs, Grand Rapids, Michigan, in 1909.

Overture, "The Festival of Youth," by The St. Louis Symphony Orchestra, under Max Zach, in St. Louis, in 1915.

"The City in the Sea," at Chicago, under Frederick Stock, in 1913.

Fantasy for pianoforte and orchestra, at New England Conservatory, Boston, soloist Lee Pattison, in 1917;
at Cleveland, soloist Heinrich Gebhard, in 1920;
at Boston, soloist Heinrich Gebhard, in 1921.

Sonata for pianoforte and violin, at Cleveland Museum of Art, by Arthur Shepherd and Arthur Beckwith, in 1924.

Overture to a Drama, first performance by Cleveland Orchestra, Arthur Shepherd conducting, in Cleveland, March 27, 1924. Cleveland Orchestra, Nikolai Sokoloff conducting, in New Haven, Poughkeepsie, and New York, in December, 1924.

"The Lord hath brought again Zion," for baritone solo, chorus and orchestra. Combined church choirs of Dayton, and Cleveland Orchestra, April 27, 1926. Nikolai Sokoloff conducting.

Program of Shepherd's concert at the home of D. S. Blossom April 21, 1926

for the festival of the Anglo-American Music Conference.

> And on that visit, to Lausanne primarily, we went down to Aubiére in France, which was the place where Arturus was stationed when he was with a band in the First World War. I shall never forget the joy of the two old people in their little walled house when they saw the *chef de musique*. Nor shall I forget the little fire on a clay hearth, perhaps three feet high, where they, with small sticks that would be thrown away in this country in two seconds, cooked an egg apiece for each of us for our food. Above the table was a basket, small, and in that basket were a few precious letters that had come from American boys to these two people in appreciation of their kindness while these men were in service.[22]

Of the works composed between 1920 and 1930 four—the Violin Sonata (c. 1916–20), *Triptych* (1925), *Horizons* (1927), and *Second Sonata* (1930)—are among Shepherd's half-dozen or so most successful compositions in point of public acceptance and performances (excluding songs). Together they comprise a second, climactic period of accomplishment surpassing his earlier prize-winning works, *Overture Joyeuse* and *Sonata for the Pianoforte.* The first two (*Triptych* under an early title) were performed at the concert, mentioned by Mrs. Shepherd, at the home of Dudley and Elizabeth Blossom in April 1926. The occasion reveals the high regard that Shepherd had earned after a residence of only six years in Cleveland. Mrs. Hughes's program, containing biographical data, a list of compositions and important performances, and graced by a photograph of Shepherd relaxing in a pastoral setting, effectively summarizes his achievements to 1926.

Probably the greatest of Shepherd's premieres, *Horizons,* performed by the Cleveland Orchestra under his direction, took place on December 15, 1927.

> "Horizons" is still referred to here and there as my most important contribution. It may be so and, in retrospect, I can return to it with considerable satisfaction. It does, I suppose, assimilate, or identify my musicality, and my various quirks, (my inherited traits, the impress of the great West and its epic—) with the notion of an American music. It is, I feel a Nature Symphony. The published title was never appropriate (I mean "Four Western pieces for symphony orchestra"). It has enough true symphonic features to merit the title 'symphony' rather than Suite. Goetschius called my attention to this long ago. I feel that the final movement "Canyons" gives cumulative significance to the whole work and for this reason I am always bothered when the two middle movements are lifted out for a concert performance.[23]

The symphony was repeated in Cleveland in 1929 and 1930, and for a few years performances were mounted in other American cities. Fabien Sevitsky took it on a European tour in 1932, conducting it in Paris, Berlin, and Warsaw. Since the Second World War it has appeared sporadically, rather stubbornly clinging to its small niche in the contemporary repertoire; and by this persistence it has become, along with *Triptych,* one of the pair of Shepherd's works through which he is most widely known.

Thus we see Shepherd, at about age fifty, well established in Cleveland, happily married, well known in the university and musical communities, and at the height of his influence as a composer. His music will change in the next twenty-five years and will not be as widely accepted as some we have discussed. Before continuing with that story, however, we digress to consider his livelihood—teaching—his thoughts about music, and his method of composing.

THE TEACHER

CHAPTER 3

By 1931 Shepherd had disengaged himself from the activities that had brought him to Cleveland—conducting the orchestra and acting as music editor and critic for the *Press*—in favor of his professorship at the university. In 1933 he was appointed chairman of the Department of Music, a position that he held until 1948, two years prior to his retirement. Here, working closely and happily with Winfred Leutner, the president of Western Reserve University, and two remarkable teachers, Arthur Quimby and Melville Smith, he fashioned a music curriculum worthy of the university. Mrs. Shepherd speaks of these associates and of the Music Department during those years:

> Arthur Quimby was in the Music Department at Western Reserve when Arturus went there. Arthur Quimby was also curator of music at the Museum. Melville Smith was at the University. I've always thought that the combination of Arthur Quimby, Melville Smith, and Arthur Shepherd was one of the greatest . . . that I have seen. Somehow or another each enhanced the others. Arthur Quimby was a peerlessly quiet, efficient administrator; and many of the cares that later became a part of Arturus' life were not present [for him] when Arthur Quimby was there. . . . I think often of those three, because somehow they created with the students of that time a whole, a comradeship, a common making of music, and a tremendously high standard of achievement. As teachers they were always present and helpful, and concerned about the music-making of the people of the department. I think the standards were terrifically high but the students loved it. . . . They did operas, as you know, with people who had no special gifts, and yet it was all held together by the standards of their musicianship and their feeling that a job well done enhanced every student who took part in it.[1]

Teaching was an ideal occupation for Shepherd, as for many American composers who have depended upon it for their livelihood. He was by nature well adapted to the reflective life, dedicated, interested, and possessed of a gift for infecting others with his own enthusiasm for music. Though mildly inclined to scholarly research, his teaching was more strongly marked by his activities as a composer and performer. He insisted on a rigorous study of fundamentals and mastery of the traditional interpretations of musical phenomena, but he was always watchful for new insights, especially the student's. He was not hesitant to depart from tradition whenever it did not square with his own experience.

Shepherd's teaching was influenced by a wide variety of musical experiences ranging from strict academicism through the spontaneous solutions of the performer to the inward searching of the composer. His undergraduate years at the New England Conservatory had exposed him to thorough traditional teaching with emphasis on correctness and technique. In work with Cutter, Faelten, and Goetschius he had acquired a deep admiration for musical masterpieces and great composers. His Salt Lake City period was spent in performance and conducting; it was then that he began seriously to compose. His association with Farwell and the Wa-Wan movement stimulated a latent, though gentle, iconoclasm in his nature and balanced his academic training with a healthy regard for contemporary music.

In the same way, his teaching maintained a balance between traditional but restrictive method and the freedom required by the more talented students who from time to time graced his classes. As a fledgling at the New England Conservatory he had been an associate of Benjamin Cutter, for whom he held a strong affection and from whom he learned much about the teacher's craft. The six years spent as conductor of the Cleveland Orchestra familiarized him in the most vivid way with the standard orchestral repertoire and were the practical basis of later classes in orchestration and composition. In the writing of lectures and program notes he not only gained a broad knowledge of many periods, composers, and styles of music, but he had also to face current musical issues and values. His steady rise through the professorial ranks at the university broadened his outlook from his classroom to the relations between his department and other disciplines, and between the university and conservatory approaches to education. He also concerned himself with questions covering the full spectrum of music education in the United States. He served on committees of the Music Teachers National Association and other organizations, and spoke at several of their conventions.

Certain books were important influences on Shepherd's teaching. For harmony and counterpoint he used Cutter's *Harmonic Analysis* and the pedagogic series by Percy Goetschius, *Elementary Counterpoint* and *Applied Counterpoint.* Though he considered the writings of Goetschius laden with minutiae and classification, he admired their logical organization and thoroughness, and acknowledged their yield for the scholar willing to mine them. For late nineteenth- and twentieth-century developments in harmony he turned to Arnold Schoenberg's *Structural Functions of Harmony* and to *The Craft of Musical Composition* by Paul Hindemith. For form, which was of special interest to him, Shepherd referred the student to Goetschius's *The Homophonic Forms of Musical Composition* and *The Larger Forms of Musical Composition.* He displayed a particular liking for the several books of Donald Francis Tovey and the *Cours de Composition* of Vincent d'Indy. He also admired the writing of Karl Eschman[2] and Ernest Toch,[3] and he frequently mentioned Abdy Williams's books *The Aristoxenian Theory of Musical Rhythm* and *The Rhythm of Modern Music.*

Here I think it is fitting to comment, if only briefly, on Shepherd's own book, *The String Quartets of Ludwig van Beethoven.* Originally prepared as separate program notes for a series of concerts in which the complete string quartets were performed, the work was of a substance deserving of publication in a more enduring form. The quartets were presented in the order of their opus numbers at seven concerts in late May and early June of 1935 in the Chamber Music Auditorium of Severance Hall. The performers were Josef Fuchs, Rudolph Ringwall, Carlton Cooley, and Victor de Gómez.

Shepherd explains in his foreword that he had "no intention, at the outset, to swell the ranks of Beethoven commentators or to add to the extensive literature already extant in this particular domain."[4] He admits, furthermore, that the work "must, of necessity, remain somewhat transitory and inconclusive."[5] His purpose was to provide, in a few pages that a concertgoer could read prior to a performance, material to increase his understanding and enjoyment of the music. It is evident that Shepherd considered his audience conversant with musical terms, forms, and to some extent styles. He included historical data and anecdotes related to the various quartets but, true to his nature, he stressed the expressive aspects of Beethoven's music. He devoted much of his space to thematic, formal, and stylistic analyses; to the growth of themes as shown in Beethoven's sketchbooks; to the relationships between themes; and other relevant aspects of the forms. The later quartets received the greater share of his attention because of their thematic interrelationships, their freedom of form, and their importance in the development of the quartet idiom. His writing reveals a penetrating study of the scores, but he also made liberal use of commentaries by Vincent d'Indy, Joseph de Marliave, Paul Bekker, and many others. For much of the research in this project Shepherd had the assistance of William S. Newman, then a student at Western Reserve University.

Books, however, were only Baedekers to Shepherd's musical adventures. The emphasis of his own study was always put squarely on the music. His most effective classroom aid was his comprehensive acquaintance with the literature. I believe, however, that the single most important influence on his teaching was his composition. It illuminated every moment of his musical life; and in the determination of all that is or is not pertinent to a musical education he followed the same criteria that guided him in composing. His teaching invariably centered on the expressive elements of music, attempting to explain not only its structure but also its communicative effect. He tried to develop "a response to those elusive factors that deal with the inner content of the music,"[6] and considered his courses merely means to this end. "Teachers fall short of their responsibilities if they don't get past the job of classifying and get over into the realm of explaining the expressive effect."[7]

The rock of Shepherd's teaching was his faith in music as an educative and cultural force. He felt that music should be a mature, confident, and indigenous art, expressive of both the reveries and the aspirations of its people—as had been so spectacularly achieved in American business, science, literature, and poetry. In his opinion American music of the mid-twentieth century had not met this challenge; and in order to raise a generation capable of doing so he nourished his students' idealistic, aesthetic, and expressive inclinations equally with their technical and scholarly skills.

Thus he hoped to prepare the soil for the growth of a really meaningful American music and to train audiences to appreciate it. "The idealistic objective should be cultural enrichment; but the cultural focus should be on our American civilization."[8]

Occasionally Shepherd was caught up in the musical rivalry between conservatories and universities. He himself had studied in the one; he had taught in both. His mature efforts had been in the university, however, and it was natural that his sympathies lay there. On occasion he discussed the responsibility of each toward its students.[9] He acknowledged the dangers inherent in the university milieu: disparity of aims and lack of uniformity between colleges, the thorny problems of credits and units (especially for performance study), and the possibility that a student might spread his energies over too many subjects to the detriment of thorough musical training and awareness of professional standards. He avoided these pitfalls by the most efficient curriculum and teaching methods he could devise; for he was, above all, convinced about the inherent opportunities and challenges offered by the university. He praised the unbounded energy and enthusiasm of college students, largely amateurs, with their open minds regarding music. He felt that a college or university music professor could make a significant contribution to American culture, and he invariably stressed the importance of securing only the most *musical* teachers for the university, men and women really able to play, conduct, compose: musicianly scholars. He argued, with a special glance at the conservatories, that a student not only be provided with the instrumental training and thorough studies in musical technique that he would need in professional life, but also be exposed to the wide variety of studies available in the arts and sciences.

> One thing is certain: the musician whose mode of expression is limited to the performing field in which virtuosity is the paramount consideration at the expense of scholarly attributes is rapidly losing out. I believe that it is not going too far to say that if through process of change and environment, the typical instrumental and vocal virtuoso should become extinct, the loss to the art of music would be practically negligible.[10]

Conversely he urged the universities to foster the purely musical skills—performance, conducting, and composition—in order that their graduates might not go forth overweight in "learning" at the expense of "muscular" musical abilities. The "half-baked musicologist" who has no performing ability was an object of his special scorn. Ideally neither scheme alone—conservatory or university—was sufficient; rather, the student needed the best of both. Together with the authorities he quoted—Otto Kinkeldey of Cornell University, George Sherman Dickinson of Vassar College, Paul Henry Lang of Columbia University, Howard Hanson of the Eastman School of Music, and Philip Greeley Clapp of the University of Iowa—he upheld the ideal of the cultured as well as the thoroughly trained musician.

As a classroom teacher Shepherd was guided by a number of fundamental precepts: (1) the distinction between analysis and synthesis, (2) a conviction that the ultimate object in the study of music is apprehension of its expressive content, (3) reliance on empirical methods derived from comparative studies, (4) a liberal attitude towards terminology, (5) a reluctance to force personal opinions on the student, (6) an attempt to develop both the written and oral powers of the student in the discussion of music, and (7) a propensity to change his courses from year to year in line with his own changing thought.

Shepherd was fond of saying, "Don't analyze until you have to, but when you have to you should know how." He considered analysis unimportant when it went no further than classification, and pernicious if done merely for its own sake. The purpose of analysis is "to sharpen the perceptions and deepen the understanding." Synthesis, on the other hand, is the extension and development of analysis into a logical and coherent description of a work, the reconstitution of analytical fragments into a meaningful whole. Synthesis involves the comparison and relation of the details of rhythm, melody, harmony, counterpoint, texture, text, and form that make up the work. The questions to be answered by synthesis are, "How does the music make sense? What is going on here? What happens in this piece that produces the expressive effect?"

Shepherd's syntheses took the form of a descriptive statement setting forth his inferences about the various phenomena of the work and the relationships between them. So far as possible he avoided analyzing to prove favored theories, for he felt that a priori analysis blinded him to unusual or unique features. He was, in fact, more interested in the uniqueness of music than in its adherence to the practice of its period. For this reason typical analytic terminology frequently did not suffice, and he was forced to coin new terms or rely on descriptive language. Knowing this, one understands his distrust of the capacities of complicated, formal, analytic systems (such as those of Goetschius and Hindemith) to apply universally to works from all periods. Shepherd allowed and even searched out examples of the elusive, the intangible, and the temporal—"the aesthetic ambiguity of a passage"—as valid factors in the creation or understanding of a work. Furthermore, he insisted that all analysis and synthesis, as for that matter all performance and composition, had to square with his ear; thus he distrusted intellectual, analytic formulations that he could not "hear." In this respect his views resemble those of Donald Francis Tovey, but Shepherd did not go so far as Tovey in suggesting that "all music must be followed phrase by phrase as a process in time."[11] As a composer he was in the habit of viewing the details of his creation not only in their relations to each other but in terms of the whole work. In analysis he was concerned also with the grand, overall view. Thus he usually scanned a piece for its large form before delving into its details. None of Shepherd's scholarly analyses are published, but his book, *The String Quartets of Ludwig van Beethoven,* and the program notes that he wrote for the Cleveland Orchestra contain fine examples at a more popular level of the method described above.

In speaking of the problems of terminology he cited a passage from Tovey:

> But the present state of musical terminology is simply not worth taking seriously; and, so long as a writer has defined his own terms and uses them consistently, the reader may, wth an easy conscience, acquiesce in Humpty Dumpty's policy of letting words mean just what he chooses, so long as he pays them extra wages for extra work.[12]

Though he required analyses (précis) from his students, Shepherd was also interested in their powers of oral expression, and to that end he provoked classroom recitations and discussions. In each case he stressed the importance of a fluent and picturesque terminology. So far as possible he avoided imposing personal views on the student, preferring freedom for individual insight and interpretation. Thus he taught more by discussion and suggestion than by lecturing.

Nevertheless, Shepherd left lengthy notes for classes in form and analysis as well as a body of materials from which we can have some knowledge of his lessons in harmony and rhythm. For composition there remains only an outline, probably the gist of an opening lecture, for a course taught in 1948–49. No subsequent daily or monthly notes have been found. He began at the student's level, requiring of beginners the study of small works of the masters and the composition of exercises similar to them. In this way he tied his work to tradition. But he also recognized that musical content conditions a form as well as filling it, and as soon as a student revealed the necessary competence Shepherd slackened his control. For really talented students he renounced a method as unnecessary. The criticism and comment of one who guides by reason of greater knowledge and experience rather than by greater talent or skill is all that is required. With such students Shepherd felt that he had indeed been successful.[13]

After his retirement he became more and more impressed with the discipline and technique, and ultimately the freedom, that come with the study of strict counterpoint by means of the five species. He cited composers who had recommended it, in particular Ernest Bloch and Ralph Vaughan Williams. He admired the results that the French conservatories obtained by this method and the good textbooks that had been organized around the species, as for example Jeppesen's *Counterpoint.*[14] He himself had not been trained in strict counterpoint, but in teaching it on occasion he had found it stimulating and valuable both for its scrutiny of the fundamental characteristics of tones and intervals and its emphasis on the behavior of the melodic line. He was especially convinced of its efficacy as a preparation for choral composition. Yet he did not advocate strict counterpoint to the exclusion of other methods; rather he believed that it should be correlated with musical analysis and freer exercises. He was also of the opinion that Merritt's rhythmically patterned cantus firmus, as opposed to the customary whole notes, was advantageous.[15]

Strongest of the elements that colored all aspects of Shepherd's teaching was the essentially musical nature of the man himself. Speculative and theoretical thinking were not foreign to him, but his forte was practical musicianship. Whether he was defending music as an appropriate subject for the college and university or the college and university as a suitable abode for music, his reasons could be reduced essentially to the importance of music as a cultural force and its effectiveness in higher education. He advocated applied and ensemble music as valid collegiate activities because of his aversion to the conception of music as a purely intellectual pursuit.[16] Nevertheless, he demanded that the performer possess an intellectual acquaintance with the history and structure of music, the better to illuminate his virtuoso technique and emotional perception.

Shepherd used any method or discipline that promised good results; and whenever a course threatened to become mechanical or to get out of touch with musical practice, he altered it. In a set of class notes one encounters an abrupt command: "Change of Tactics! The Spirit rather than the letter!" He was demanding and thorough, but his demands required a sharpening of musical acumen and understanding rather than the acceptance of dogma, and his coverage was flexible rather than fixed. Broadly speaking, his method emphasized an empirical approach, comparative studies, and ultimate reliance on musical masterworks.

THOUGHTS ABOUT MUSIC

CHAPTER 4

Extended contemplation of a composer's music stimulates curiosity about his own sentiments concerning it and all music. Were J. S. Bach's five cycles of cantatas for the church year merely the natural product of a conscientious and supremely gifted craftsman in the fulfillment of his contract? Or was the artist in Bach continually and consciously speaking? This curiosity leads us to the letters and biographies of composers in a fascinating study not only of their music, but of their minds and the conditions in which they worked. As with all composers, Arthur Shepherd's thoughts and feelings about music were deeply rooted in his personality and experiences. Moreover, he was fond of discussing his art, which enables us to examine many of his ideas and opinions.

He sometimes opened lectures on the general nature of music with a quotation from some recently read or remembered author; for example, Combarieu's definition, "Music is the art of thinking in sounds"[1] and Tovey's aphorism, "Music is neither a game nor a science; it is a language."[2] He was fond of relating music to other fields and, again following Jules Combarieu, he described its common boundaries with acoustics, physiology, mathematics, psychology, aesthetics, history, philology, paleography, and sociology. In considering the composer's experience, he stressed the nonverbal nature of the mental activity required in musical composition and performance.

> Now the generally accepted definition of thinking is the "uniting of *concepts*" which, in turn, implies the use of words. "The earth turns round the sun" or "The street car runs by electricity." The originality of the musician consists of suppressing the concepts in the acts of the intelligence, that is, he *does succeed* in thinking without the use of words. It is like a free act of nature.[3]

Tovey's definition of music just quoted led Shepherd to conclude that music fulfills its purpose only when something expressive and meaningful is communicated to a knowledgeable and sympathetic (or at least understanding) audience. He believed that an audience is essential to complete the artistic function, and it was on the basis of its communication with an audience that he judged and criticized music, his own as well as that of others. He regarded the lack of such an audience to be "the most fundamental deterrent to the development of a vital American music."[4]

Concomitant with the idea of music as a communicative art is the necessity of evaluating its truth, or integrity.

> We may find one ready and valuable criterion for distinguishing true music from false. If in our appreciation of it the reason plays no part, if we are not conscious of any fineness of style, or organic completeness of structure, but are merely tasting a series of unrelated and independent sounds, then that music for us has no meaning and no right to its title.[5]

Though he himself quoted this passage of Sir Henry Hadow, in which the "truth" of a work is determined on essentially intellectual grounds, Shepherd's own judgment seems to have been more intuitive than reasoned. "The truth and expressiveness of genius is always communicative," he wrote. "I have used here the word 'truth' which I have long felt to be applicable, perhaps mysteriously so, to those moments, those periods, those combinations which stir us deeply."[6]

This pastoral photograph of Shepherd appeared in the Blossom recital program pictured on page 20.

Shepherd regarded musical compositions as he did other phenomena of God's creation, and he looked upon his study of them as similar to the naturalist's observations of animals, flowers, and trees.

> For my part, I can no more be skeptical of the worth of the naive tunes of Schubert's Waltzes and Deutsche [Tänze] than I can of the daisies that grow up in my yard. I can be no more skeptical of the songs and chamber music and symphonies of Schubert than I can of the sun, moon and stars.[7]

That he was able to classify musical works by types did not blind Shepherd to their uniqueness. It was this which most interested him and which he emphasized in his discussion of music.

Thus, in Shepherd's basic attitudes toward music one notes that: (1) music is an art; (2) music is concerned not only with the emotions but also with the intelligence, and is the art of thinking in sound; (3) music is both expressive and communicative; (4) music is related to other fields of knowledge; (5) music can be judged, according to its effect upon us, as true or false; and (6) music has many characteristics of natural phenomena—though it is manmade, it resembles works of nature.

AESTHETICS, ATTITUDES, MUSICAL EDUCATION

> If one must pick and choose, I'll put it this way: *J. S. Bach* is my first love but my favorite composer is Bahaymobeeschub.[8]
>
> Now you raise the question IV about literature *on* music—Schweitzer,[9] Spengler,[10] Sorokin[11] *et al.* as shaping forces in my *aesthetic attitude.* But bless your soul I don't believe that I have an "*aesthetic attitude.*" I have only the desire and urge to fulfill as best I may, my destiny as a *musician.* That's a big order, and as yet very insufficiently accomplished. I can dream of a *Kind* of music, more self-sufficient, more pure, less introspective (I wouldn't say "abstract") than anything that I have written. Whether, considering my individual make-up, my environment, and the spirit of the times, this can ever be accomplished, cannot be foretold.
>
> *Least* of all, am I a fashion chaser or a fashion monger. I am full of admiration and confidence for the host of young American composers of talent and competence. Some of them well on their way to significant achievement; some of them not sufficiently independent of the fashion parade.
>
> I doubt that there was ever a period of history when the hand of destiny weighed so heavily on a leading world nation as now presses down on the America of today; or that a challenge so clamorous and magnificent was hurled at a people born in traditions of freedom.
>
> How is it conceivable that American creative artists can become detached or segregated from these forces of destiny to the extent that he concern himself mainly with laboratory techniques or hair-splitting aesthetics?
>
> Now from all this you will, I hope, get a fairly clear notion of my credo, or should I say of my *aspirations!*[12]

It may be said that the essential qualities of a composer are aspiration, awareness, and technique. None of these may be slighted; each brings indispensable ingredients to the composer's art. On the basis of these qualities Shepherd again and again counseled the composer "to be *Himself*; to cultivate *Himself*; to express *Himself*; to trust in God and his fellow-man; to look into his heart and Write."[13] Such an attitude, aided by the scrupulous development of a commanding technique, will never mislead him. Should genius also be present the art will be incalculably enriched.

The success of the great composers whose genius has solved the artistic problems of their time heartened Shepherd against the prophets of doom in our day. He believed that history is fashioned by big men. His confidence in the inevitable appearance of genius made him optimistic for the future of American music. He also knew that in most cases the work of a genius grows in soil tilled by his predecessors, and therefore he valued the music of all sincere composers of more modest gifts. He was able to repudiate the American habit of artistic self-incrimination, our cultural inferiority complex as evidenced in our tendency continually to explain our work to ourselves and others. He preached the goodness and the soundness, if not the greatness, of American music; and asked merely for a hearing, for the nourishment of an audience such that genius, when it appeared, would be recognized.

Being a composer, Shepherd made little claim to be a master theorist or teacher, though I think it possible that his considerable talents in these fields were sometimes detrimental to his composing. A composer's preoccupation with his work robs him of the time needed to keep up with advances in all parts of the musical community. To Hindemith's remark that composers are not necessarily good theorists,[14] Shepherd retorted, "It is still more seldom that theorists are good composers, and it is equally obvious that composers are notoriously untrustworthy as aestheticians."[15] Nevertheless a composer usually must teach to make a living and, as Hindemith points out, his inherent creative gifts are a great asset in the classroom. His problem is to balance the time required to make his teaching effective with the time needed for composing, which is his overriding responsibility.

For the general musician Shepherd stressed the development of selectivity, evaluation, curiosity, and objectivity in analysis. He advocated equally historical and aesthetic studies, technical analysis, and performance training. He urged students not only to assimilate tradition but to rely on their curiosity, not only to classify but to search out the unique, not only to specialize but to range widely and experience much, not only to manipulate materials already mastered but to reach beyond their grasp.

> As practical and practicing musicians your sensitivity and curiosity should prompt you to tackle any problem of analysis incident to the happenings and the "goings-on" in music.[16]

"Let the music have its way with you," he said. After the analysis, talk, discussion, aesthetic speculation, quest for meaning, and attempt to explain the artistic experience have failed, as they probably are bound to fail, return to the listening, reading, performing, and composing of music. It will be more meaningful for the attempt to explain it, but all else is meaningless without the music.

HIS OWN MUSIC

Shepherd's urge to write, common to all composers, manifested itself in at least two ways. There were times and compositions for which he felt a strong impulse to work, a stimulus urging him to expression. *Horizons,* for example, grew from a desire to write of his Western heritage, of the locale and spirit of the place where he was born and its people. Other big works emerged from similar motives: *Overture to a Drama* and the Violin Sonata are two of these. In like manner Shepherd developed a lively response to the mystical philosophy of Rabindranath Tagore's poetry during the composition of *Triptych,* though the work had its genesis in a commission for a chamber composition including voice.

This need for expression was not, however, an indispensable factor in his work. Shepherd also composed on a day-to-day basis, in which the momentum was maintained not so much by emotional prods as by the desire to keep busy, to explore a certain form or medium, to set an appealing text, or to work out a series of harmonic and melodic ideas. The motivation of much of his work was the desire to remain active and to extend his technique. The music written from this motive was as important to him, and thus as carefully turned and highly regarded, as that which had more specifically emotional beginnings. He mentioned the second piano sonata in this connection.

> The important thing is the vitality of the idea behind the composition. Poetic materials can vitalize an impulse—words do this for some composers. Who shall say in a quartet, symphony, sonata, or whatnot, what the real impulse back of it may be?[17]

Shepherd was inclined to think that Brahms felt a stronger impulse and challenge in the composition of the First Symphony than the Second. Likewise, with regard to a point raised at the beginning of this chapter, he believed that whereas many of Bach's works undoubtedly sprang from deeply religious feelings, others must have come about simply through the exercise of his artistry. Nevertheless, the origin of a work was not Shepherd's vital interest, but its quality, and he was not distracted by the difficulties in correlating these different though perhaps related aspects of it. He had great faith in the effectiveness of a daily routine for "getting things done." A composition is written through sustained, steady effort as much as by inspiration. A byproduct of continual activity is technique. For Shepherd art was something to grow in, and the improvement of his technique was an incentive that spurred him to study music and put notes on paper until the very end of his life. Perhaps this elucidates the enthusiasm, the youthful approach to life and work, that impressed his friends as one of the inherent qualities of his personality.

Arthur Shepherd (center) discusses a point of musical interpretation with Beryl Rubinstein (seated at piano) as Herbert Elwell (right) listens.

STYLE

The style of a composer's work is one of his fundamental problems, and Shepherd's convictions about style were marked by struggle. Most of his music was founded basically on two propositions discussed above: (1) the best music is both expressive and communicative, and (2) the composer should concern himself more with what he finds within than with efforts to be up-to-date in his utterance. He did not mean that in being communicative one need be naive, nor that in looking within he could afford to ignore other new music. One cannot evade the responsibility to study and evaluate significant modern trends and to consider those features of fresh styles commensurate with his purposes and aesthetics. It is a formidable duty, demanding of time and energy, but it is necessary for any composer who meditates on the relationship between his work and the time in which he lives and who wishes his music to express not only himself but his culture and environment.

In resolving this problem Shepherd followed his own advice: "to be *Himself;* to cultivate *Himself;* to express *Himself.* . . ."[18] His inability to renounce expression and communication in art explains his retention of consonance. Though he denied himself no dissonance, and his music at times is quite dissonant, he also needed consonance and the resources of tonality for the direction and fulfillment of his ideas. In his view the avant-garde styles of his day revealed not only their attraction to dissonance but equally their abhorrence of consonance. He often mentioned that new music had destroyed more of musical technique than it had created: "It is difficult to hold to the restrictions of modernism."[19] A product of his particular time and generation and of his adoptive eclectic, sophisticated, and academic New England culture, Shepherd could never seriously have embraced dodecaphony. He did not proscribe it for others; he was merely dubious about its ability to measure up to his requirements. Use of the twelve-tone method is a matter that each composer must settle for himself, "and take the consequences." Regardless of how far afield his musical speculations took him, traditional concepts of melody, harmony, and structure, though altered and stretched to the limits of recognition, could not be discarded. He was therefore a traditionalist. His own definition, stated in a lecture, bears out this view:

> Tradition.
> What is there about this word that is so provocative? What do we mean when we employ it in conversation and in writing? Is it a derogatory epithet or is it the acknowledgement of some recognizable achievement?
> One hears the phrase such and such a work is "in the great tradition," one hears also the phrase, such and such a person is a "slave to tradition."
> Now by connotation and implication "tradition" is inseparable from our noblest concepts. God Himself is our greatest tradition: Truth is traditional; our habits of speech, food, clothing, are traditional, our Democratic Ideals are traditional. Great works of art are the means of establishing tradition. . . .
> The connotations of the word are preponderantly good and constructive. And yet it seems inherent in human destiny to contend and battle, resist and break away from traditional practices.
> This is particularly observable in the realm of art. But this apparent strife is basically nothing more than the normal operation of the laws which govern growth and change. So, I think we may assume that a "traditionalist" is one who creates with an awareness of his heritage and an awareness of doctrine and discipline.[20]

In Shepherd's view it is a trend of our times to relate music to science, to create arithmetically, "which is, in effect, a transference from one realm to another."[21] It was his view that the "mechanistic" varieties differ from the "artistic" modes of composition more in kind than in degree, but that—even if one granted that Schoenberg's serialism was but a method—for him it lacked expression. Thus he had to consider it antithetical to artistic communication. It is not difficult to understand his hope that music might perhaps get back to older premises. He found it ironic that Schoenberg, in justifying his own complexities, had appealed to the music of Brahms.[22] Though Shepherd conceded that Brahms's music is frequently intricate, especially in its rhythms, he felt that it invariably proves itself by its expressiveness, its essentially spiritual content and ability to communicate. On the whole Schoenberg's music did not speak to him directly, yet he acknowledged his delight with certain of the master's works, particularly *Pierrot Lunaire,* which he considered extraordinary and ideally expressive of its subject. Nonetheless, I believe that he was unconvinced by Schoenberg's account of the gradual increase of chromaticism, the emancipation of dissonance, and the evolution of serial technique at the beginning of the twentieth century. I doubt that he accepted Schoenberg's assertion that serial music was inevitable and hence traditional, or that its aim was greater comprehensibility. For Shepherd tradition required tonality, thematicism, and perceptible form. Thus he always constructed his music out of themes and subjects.

Many of Shepherd's themes can be described as tuneful. Newman writes of this element in his style:

> Even more important to an understanding of his style is his conspicuous success as a melodist. He is at his best when he hits on a good tune. Good borrowed tunes are the very heart of the second and third movements of his *Horizons,* his organ *Fantasia on "The Garden Hymn,"* and his orchestral *Fantasia on Down East Spirituals.* Most often his original melodies are folkish and modal in character. His favorite modal inflections appear to be the lowered second and raised fourth. "There must be a strong atavistic streak somewhere in my system," he writes in a recent letter, "for I catch myself writing tunes with a pronounced Celtic flavor."[23] As far back as 1907 an excellent folk-like tune, reminiscent of Gottschalk's best, appears with abrupt vigor in the finale of his prize-winning First Piano Sonata, a work that displays a surging youthful drive and precocious command of the then newest harmony. . . .
> Harmonized in character, tunes of this sort opened the way for Shepherd, as for many another composer, to the frank simplicity and directness, that good taste forbade him to find in the embers of dying Romanticism. By the same token, they have also answered his need for melody more successfully than any of the newer, less traditional tonal means.[24]

To Newman's list of pieces which make use of borrowed themes we can add the Second Symphony (1938), which has a Mexican cowboy song in the Trio of the Scherzo, and the theme of the second movement of the Violin Sonata, which was suggested to Shepherd by a popular song of the time, a song that he could no longer identify when I was discussing it with him. The tune which carries the finale of the First Piano Sonata, that reminds Newman of Gottschalk, is not an original melody but was first heard by Shepherd as a part of the incidental music to the traveling play *The Virginian* while he was conducting the pit orchestra in the Salt Lake Theater.[25]

Shepherd was not hesitant to acknowledge, and if necessary defend, his fondness for tunes:

> How comes it that so tuneful a composer as Schubert grows rather than shrinks in importance with the passing years? Some may dispute my characterization of the present as a "tuneless" epoch. But it would seem that most of the good tunes are out in the back yard, so to speak, and one has to go slumming to get them.[26]

As tunefulness is on the whole an element of his themes, so is thematic material the foundation of his forms. He was painstaking in its creation. He worked it hard "to squeeze the juice out of the theme, rhythmically as well as every other way."[27] Conversely he was skeptical of attempts to analyze or write music without themes. He feared that athematic techniques would obliterate the landmarks by which we perceive and appreciate musical forms; and he resisted theory or analysis that hinted at such possibilities as, for example, Roger Sessions's remarks to the effect that compositions, even sonatas, that are not built upon themes can be found among the classics.[28]

Shepherd did not usually work toward a preconceived form, yet his music reveals the control and organization one expects of a composer with his prodigious knowledge of Classic and Romantic music. In his work one finds sonata forms, ternaries, and other common types as well as freer structures that mix the characteristics of two or more of the older forms or that derive from empirical procedures. Thus he combined the lessons of historical models with an innovator's speculation. To state it the other way around, he claimed the freedom to do as he pleased, but he was influenced by tradition. For example, in speaking about his Fourth String Quartet he said:

> The first movement is done. I am at present working on the last; but this time, in contrast to my usual method, I have been working on all the movements simultaneously. I am much interested in the organic relationships between the movements. The slow movement is pretty well done and a scherzo is in process, although I have not yet decided whether or not to have a scherzo. I think I probably will because certain aspects of the first movement seem to demand it.[29]

How was he achieving unity in the whole of the piece? Was he using cyclic form as in other works?

> Well, cyclical process is a consequence of the use of the materials. It's not that one sets out necessarily to write in cyclical form. The device results from constant consideration of the motives and other materials. Vivien Slater played that beautiful A Major Sonata, Op. 101 of Beethoven, and I pointed out a figuration in the third movement that is really the theme of the first movement. I wonder if it was conscious with Beethoven, or if it does not merely represent another manifestation of his preoccupation with his materials. That type of analysis that goes into such tiny detail about the derivation of everything goes against my grain—like Reti[30] for instance.
>
> I think it is very important to recognize that, whereas a composer normally uses materials consciously, sometimes they creep in unconsciously. How to determine which is which from the music would be difficult.[31]

How does one choose key relationships? "By ear," he answered. "It comes from a highly developed sense of tonality and harmonic instinct—from a commitment to, and assimilation of, harmonic principles. Sometimes it is conscious, sometimes not."[32]

In one of his letters written during the composition of *A Psalm of the Mountains*,[33] he said:

> Now I must be off to my studio. My writing goes at snail pace. My ears are pretty bad.[34] I haven't even finished that choral setting of Judge Allen's poem but I know quite well how it will shape up. Even now, near the end, I could use a few more words to round out a fugato section, but I haven't the crust to approach Her Honor with this outrageous notion,[35] so I suppose I shall have to go on reiterating "Before thy steadfast strength my feeble fears pass as a breath on glass."
>
> You see, I don't want the composition to run out of "breath." This: breathing space, is I believe a basic factor and problem in any and all vocal composition; choral or solo-setting.[36]

All this indicates Shepherd's concern for the form of his music. Undoubtedly much of his writing was instinctive, quickly laid out. The tonal and thematic coherence of his large compositions show that his thought and talent naturally encompassed large ideas, large subjects, and large forms. In spite of this facility, however, he did not compose in a torrent. After the heart had made a beginning, the head and hand subjected the work to the scrutiny of unrelenting technical self-criticism. Shepherd's workmanship, which was of a high order, stemmed from continual reappraisal and refinement, processes that went on even after the first performance of a work, for he frequently rewrote passages that did not come off according to his expectations.

THE CASE AGAINST SHEPHERD

There are many reasons why Shepherd's music has not been widely successful, not the least of which is the relatively greater prominence gained by other talented composers of his day. It will not discredit anyone's music to suggest that Shepherd's is worthy of more attention than it receives. It fails partly because it is not in the advanced styles that today's knowledgeable performers and audiences expect when contemporary music is programmed. Though his experimental and mature works are closer to their time than one who is familiar only with his most successful compositions would expect, he did not keep up with the latest manifestations of musical thought as they appeared through the first half of the twentieth century.

Our sense of values can sometimes be so affected by the knowledge of dates and circumstances surrounding music that we may hesitate to show enthusiasm over new works that shun contemporary idiom. An assessment of new music may be obstructed by its propinquity, a lack of familiarity with it, and perhaps an eagerness not to be late in acknowledging its importance. We have a right to distrust our emotions; immediate appeal does not necessarily indicate quality. Yet it is regrettable if we altogether reject emotion, for an unconditioned response to their music is what most composers surely would hope to command.

If a man writes beyond his audience he can appeal to the future, but in the present he is, in his own view, right, and can adopt the attitude that others simply do not understand him. Another who, to satisfy himself, must try to be communicative has thereby dropped his guard and, being "understood," is open to dismissal even though by his own standards he is successful. He can only hope that eventually excellence will be recognized, regardless of idiom. In the swamping abundance of music in this era, when success hangs partly on fashion, Shepherd's music can only rise through the intercession of influential artists who are willing to reveal its beauties sufficiently often that its natural vitality can gain the momentum necessary to lift it into the repertoire—to draw it airborne, so to speak.

Arthur Shepherd's music has also attracted its share of unfavorable criticism. Perhaps the most damaging published critique is that of Denoe Leedy, who contended that, except for *Horizons*, Shepherd's forms and works exhibit a sameness in harmony, melody, and form—"the same attitude towards solving constructive problems, if not the same solutions"—that points to mere reproductive activity rather than continually new creative effort.[37] To some extent this is true. Shepherd's songs, for example, tend toward similarity of mood; and the differences in general effect between some of the *Eclogues* and *Exotic Dances* (see Part 3) for piano are not great. On the other hand, the "sameness" in Shepherd's works is but little removed from the "unity of style" exhibited by other composers. Furthermore, differences in melody, harmony, form, and texture occurred over the years. By and large, that music for which he is unfavorably criticized is the relatively successful music of the twenties, the best known and most readily available. Few are acquainted with the manuscript works in which many of his best pages are hidden. One cannot help wondering if Leedy intended to include in his criticism such pieces as *Gigue Fantasque, Invitation to the Dance*, or *Reverie*,* all of which were in manuscript at the time he was writing.

Yet Shepherd has written bad pages and pages of little interest—pages that raise the question, "What for?" and pages that in another's music would elicit his own comment: "You don't get your money's worth." Some of these are published. The teaching piece *Autumn Fields* (1935), for example, is so different from his usual style, so conventional—even trite—that one wonders why he released it. For me it lacks the delicious charm of which teaching pieces are capable, exemplified in Béla Bartók's *Mikrokosmos* or similar works of Pál Kadosa. It resembles a counterpoint exercise from one of his classes rather than an original product.

Along with others, Leedy suggested that Shepherd frequently wrote too many notes and that his scores are cluttered, needlessly difficult, and complex. The piano music can be treacherous to read—it is frequently filled with arpeggiated and interlocking patterns, burdened with sustained tones impossible to play as written with either hands or pedals, and sometimes exasperatingly inconsistent in notation. But once learned, the music lies under the fingers. It is the formidable façade of his music—its abstruseness, the problem of finding out what it is all about, and the practice required to get at the idea—that tempt one to lay it aside unlearned and unperformed.

Another difficulty with regard to both his music and his relations with others was Shepherd's pronounced faculty for criticism. He could put his finger on the strong and weak spots of a work virtually at a single reading or hearing. But Leedy marks a curious inconsistency: "His magnificent critical acumen, so powerful when applied to the other person's music, frequently forsakes him" in a composition of his own.[38] He cites weaknesses, such as Shepherd's tendency to remain too long within one key, as evidence of a lack of critical perception while composing. The detection of faults frequently arises from differences of opinion, but it is true that his critical talent caused Shepherd grief. It slowed him down and probably generated some of the complexity mentioned above. He "frequently indulges in just plain tonal suicide, mulling over his materials to the point where there is nothing left of the original artistic impulse."[39]

One finds this "mulling over" in his propensity for revision. Surely Shepherd revised too often. In his quest for perfection he made it virtually impossible for us to decide which versions of certain works are preferable. His critical acumen, far from being impotent for his own music, was too active over it. It reflects a strange insecurity, as though he were unable to make up his mind about the final shape of a work. This vacillation was evident in the thirties as he experimented with new devices: one piece contained new things, another was a throwback to the tried and true; and the next moment he was writing to Goetschius that he could not give up this or that, as though he wished he were someone else. Performers were annoyed by his habit of tampering with the music, even to the extent of making last-minute changes during the final rehearsals before performance. Some were reluctant to play for him, feeling that he was inflexible in his opinions and driven by an inordinate desire for perfection. Undoubtedly his set and forceful opinions generated friction from time to time. His views in the controversy over the selection of a conductor for the Cleveland Orchestra in 1943 were well reasoned and eloquent, but extreme and contrary to those of persons closer to the seat of decision.[40] His support of the university as an ideal center for the teaching and study of music was energetic; and, intentionally or not, he needled advocates of the conservatory plan, closest of whom were the faculty of the Cleveland Institute of Music.

In my opinion the neglect of Shepherd's music arises from a combination of these factors and the general disinterest in serious American music that is noticeable in our land. Even the most successful composers must feel at times that they are in competition not so much with each other or with contemporary Europeans as they are with the Classic and Romantic writers whose works make up the bulk of our programs. It is ironic that at Shepherd's death the Cleveland Orchestra performed in his honor—in memory of one who, in recognition of a long career and justifiable achievements, eminently merited the appellation of "dean of Cleveland composers"[41]—not his own music, but the *Tragic Overture* of Johannes Brahms.

Shepherd was aware of these problems and shortcomings as well as many others that bore upon his situation: a paucity of publications and recordings,[42] the lack of a champion performer, and so on. It was to his disadvantage that he could not or would not promote his music more effectively. It was probably within his power to write so that his music would attract more attention—he had, perhaps, exaggerated notions of musical and personal integrity. Probably many obstacles to success resulted from an overstrict, uncompromising adherence to an outmoded idea of the right, the true, and the beautiful. Nevertheless he believed in himself and in his music. He spoke when he felt something had to be said, and it was evidently more important to him that his works accurately reflect his views on art than that they spread his name in concert halls far and wide. To him, notes represented more than tunes and scintillating harmonies. Shepherd's notes spoke the language of his heart and soul, and the thoughts they uttered are true to his whole philosophy and being. Thus, like Schoenberg, Shepherd *had* to write as he did; but, unlike the Viennese master, he was a conservative.

One of the gifts of time to any composer's work is perspective; eventually, his compositions must be judged on their own merits rather than against the popular demands of their time. In Shepherd's case the transitional nature of our musical era—full of flux, variety, offshoots, and dead ends—could work to his advantage. If the divergent philosphies of today's music never reconverge, people may come to accept individual musics, just as they accept different nationalities or personalities, and audiences may fragment to follow numerous paths. One of these, I hope, will lead back to the eclectic Americans of the first half of our century. Perhaps then Shepherd and his music will take their rightful place.

WORDS AND MUSIC

CHAPTER 5

We have followed Shepherd from his Western beginnings through his conservatory days in Boston, his early professional career in Salt Lake City, and his activities back in Boston as a teacher and composer, together with the hiatus of his military service in France during World War I. We have followed him to Cleveland, where he was part of the newly formed orchestra and where he gradually rose through the academic ranks to his position as professor of music at Western Reserve University. We have discussed his music, his teaching, and his thoughts about music. But much about his life and work remains to be told.

In Part Two of this book, Shepherd's compositional techniques will be discussed in detail. Those analyses will be of interest mainly to musicians who are caught up in matters of technique and style; they are unavoidably technical and probably somewhat dry. However, the *ways* in which Shepherd composed can be described in everyday terms—and that is the task of this chapter. I have used his vocal pieces as my vehicle because they, and the songs in particular, were of special interest to him—close to him—and he often talked about them. The things he said also apply with only slight changes of emphasis to the rest of his work.

From 1905 to 1922 Arthur Shepherd's compositions always included vocal music. After the period from 1922 to 1931, when he wrote only instrumental works, he resumed the composition of songs and choral works, completing about two every year until 1951 when his activity in all categories declined. Three final vocal works appeared in his last period, 1955–57. Particularly productive years were 1909, when the *Five Songs,* Op. 7, on poems by James Russell Lowell, were published by the Wa-Wan Press; 1926; 1931–32; and especially 1941, by far the busiest year of Shepherd's creative life.

As a whole Shepherd's songs are representative of the modally touched, diatonic music elsewhere described, and for this reason I shall discuss them all together. One might ask why his vocal music should be more restrained in technique and range of expression and less disposed toward the experiments of the thirties than were his instrumental works. First, I believe, it was because he held to conventional conceptions of vocal music—well-defined voice types and ranges, steady legato voice production, and a tuneful melody with relatively diatonic intervals. The wide skips, chromaticism, and vague tonality that lie so easily under the pianist's fingers did not strike Shepherd as promising vocal procedures. Second, since he was drawn largely to lyric poetry, he did not face the extreme and dramatic subjects that might have engendered more radical musical devices, as, for example, Schoenberg's *Pierrot Lunaire,* with which Shepherd was familiar. Furthermore, by his method of adapting words to music he derived the musical rhythms from the text itself, a practice that closed many avenues of rhythmic experimentation.

A knowledge of Shepherd's method of composing throws light upon the nature of his songs. Music was generally always eddying about in his head. Sometimes it took the form of a simple tune repeating itself, irritating in its insistence; but at other times all the various motives of a new piece to which he was committed jostled for his attention.

Yes, sometimes I get my head so full of ideas that I just have to sit down at a table, clear out the confusion and get down the rhythmic and melodic outlines. Rhythmic flow and melodic motivation—these are more important in the early stages than the harmony. I often get bogged down in detail and have trouble sketching fast enough, keeping up the flow.[1]

I was in and out of the studio during the composition of Shepherd's choral work *A Psalm of the Mountains* (1956). He wrote at a table before a window, his back to the piano. In the evenings when I was working there alone I would often pass the sketch resting on the music rack of the instrument where he had last used it. It reminded me of a phrase he sometimes used to describe his work: "Just ruminating over it." There were sketches on the page, here and there a bit of text with a few notes on the staff or rhythmic patterns beneath, a measure or two spaced out for the accompaniment with the rhythms written in. Shepherd's settings often blossomed out of heightened, expressive recitations of the poem; these suggested to him not only the pace and rhythm of the melody, the phrase lengths, high and low tones, and climaxes, but also the motives, the returns to prior materials, the musical references between voice and accompaniment, and so forth. Thus the text was the form-producing element. The first stage of writing consisted of a study of the poem for its meaning and rhythmic characteristics and the noting down of those musical ideas that immediately suggested themselves to him. This gave him a sketchy perception of the total shape—as yet no more than a feeling for the nature, mood, and scope of the work. A perfect and poignant illustration of an unfinished composition at this stage of its creation is this facsimile of Shepherd's copy of a poem by James Joyce, found on the desk after his death.[2] Looking at this sketch one is reminded of his remark that "in all my vocal compositions, the matter of prosody and all rhythmical features should claim first attention. . . ." In the second stage of composition he completed the music. At any point, however, something new might intrude, deflecting him from the charted course.

Though the form that eventually materialized from this text-derived procedure was frequently unique—for Shepherd wasted no time in consciously reproducing traditional patterns—he insisted that it be musically self-sufficient. Despite its textual derivation it had to make musical sense. Shepherd worked for a delicate balance between these compositional forces. He admired and often cited the balance of text and music in the songs of Schubert, where one finds all the musical implications worked out in a most natural way within the conditioning spirit of the poem. Indeed, he stood in awe of Schubert's miraculous ability to illuminate a poem through melodic line with extraordinary economy of instrumental support.

Shepherd loved poetry and naturally worked with poems from which he experienced a lively response. Though he was very sensitive to word rhythms and prosody he did not require specific rhythmic modes or versification. He usually sought poems whose lyrical quality was pronounced, and he was pleased when an occasional declamatory passage was present for emotional relief and musical contrast. He did not attempt to overcome difficult lines in otherwise attractive poems, but would simply turn to another. He also avoided works heavy with philosophic or psychological implications (as an example he mentioned the poetry of Ezra Pound) because he could not assimilate in a short song their weighty content. He was particularly fond of the Irish poets Oliver St. John Gogarty and James Stephens.[3]

Who goes amid the green wood
With Springtide all adorning her
Who goes amid the merry green wood
To make it merrier?

Who passes in the s unlight
By ways that know the light footfall?
Who passes in the sweet sunlight
With mien so virginal?

The ways of all the woodland
Gleam with a soft and golden fire
For whom does all the sunny woodland
Carry so brave attire?

O, it is for my true love
The woods their rich apparel wear
O, it is for my own true love,
That is so young and fair.

WINDS OF MAY, THAT DANCE ON THE SEA,
DANCING A RING*AROUND IN GLEE
FROM FURROW TO FURROW, WHILE OVERHEAD
THE FOAM FLIES UP TO BE GARLANDED,
IN SILVERY ARCHES SPANNING THE AIR
SAW YOU MY TRUE LOVE ANYWHERE?
WELLADAY! WELLADAY!
FOR THE WINDS OF MAY!
LOVE IS UNHAPPY WHEN LOVE IS AWAY!

James Joyce

In addition to the rhythm and meaning of a poem, Shepherd studied the vowel sounds on which he would found his vocal line. He delighted in recitation, his voice prolonging the vowels to accentuate their length and roundness. He rolled out syllables from word to word in a gentle, stately rhythm, using canorous resonance and undulating, high, impassioned pitch which lowered and softened as he approached a cadence.

From Mantua's meadows to imperial Rome
Came Virgil, with the woodlight in his eyes;
Browned by the suns that round his hillside home
Burned on the chestnuts and the ilices.[4]

"What a wonderful poem," he said. "Listen to the *m*'s, and vowels in the first line—and to the *o*'s in the third line: '*Browned* by the suns that *round* his hillside *home.*' " His mouth formed the *o* as he broadened and savored the vowels. Study of this sort assured the effective utilization of each word and vowel. Shepherd had steeped himself in the accentuation and rhythmic treatment of the text in great songs and in the larger works and writings of accomplished practitioners of the art—Richard Wagner, for one, and Arnold Schoenberg, whose *Sprechstimme* captivated him. He was impressed by the use of *Sprechstimme* in Alban Berg's *Wozzeck,* particularly admiring its ability to project the words over the orchestra.

Shepherd labored to ensure that the texts with which he worked would be recognized and understood. He was especially careful about the overlapping of words or lines in choral music. He believed that close reiteration of syllables was not only detrimental to one's comprehension but ugly whenever it emphasized any sibilants or hard consonants.

I suggest that it would be very much worth your while to look closely into this feature by scrutinizing certain choral works of the Masters. Sure enough, you'll find a good many passages where these conflicting over-laps occur in contrapuntal writing; for example in the 5th measure of the 2nd *Kyrie Eleison* of Bach's B minor Mass (last syllable of Elei*son*) and later on, the first syllable of *K*yrie on successive beats between Sop[rano] and Bass.

In Handel's "Messiah" (in the florid contrapuntal passages) there are very few instances of these conflicting overlaps. There is, however, in No. 35, "Let All the Angels," a glaring example:

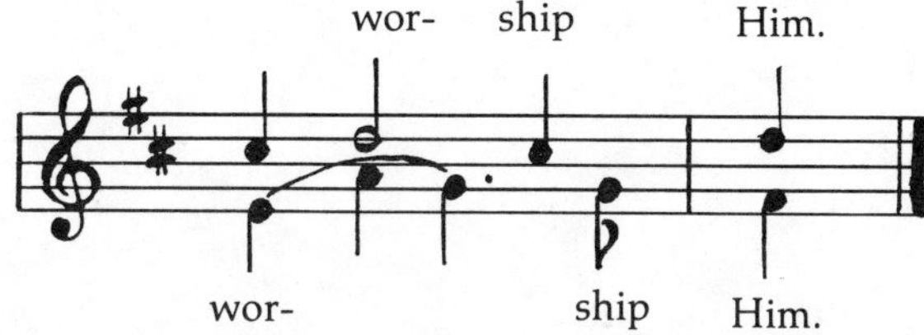

The point I wish to make is that regardless of the comparative frequency of these conflicts, they ought to be scrupulously avoided *whenever possible.*[5]

His songs also reveal a fastidious concern over the problem of fitting the musical form to the poem. He saw it as a matter of scope, of designing the music to round out, satisfy, and complete itself within the framework of the text. We have already seen how this troubled him in the composition of *A Psalm of the Mountains.*[6] Although he recognized text repetition to be a traditional device of choral music, he personally preferred to view the music and words together as the more significant structure. He was reluctant to repeat words simply for the sake of greater musical length.

Shepherd's accompaniments, whether for piano or ensemble, rarely duplicate the vocal melody; instead they provide motivic and contrapuntal comment. When an instrument doubles the melody it is for a few notes only, after which it separates again from the voice. One gains the impression of two distinct melodies occasionally and briefly united. On the other hand, when he saw difficult skips or entrances in the solo part, Shepherd liked to provide one or two guide notes in the accompaniment as cues for the singer.

Certain textures that are rare in Shepherd's solo piano music will be found in his song accompaniments. One is the device of sweeping arpeggios.[7] Others may be found in the accompaniments of *Softly Along the Road of Evening, When Rooks Fly Homeward** (1941), and *Most Quietly at Times**; these have textures in which quiet, separately stemmed, contrapuntal parts of independent yet similar and coordinated rhythms combine to produce almost homophonic effects.

Since Shepherd drew his music out of the text it is not surprising that many of his songs are through-composed—that is, set in forms freely shaped in response to the text rather than musically shaped according to traditional thematic and tonal patterns. The unity that they exhibit arises out of a consistency of texture and motivic shapes rather than recurrent themes and phrases.[8] When a text returned to the original mood or first line it was natural for him to return to the original music. Occasionally, therefore, he produced vocal works in ternary form,[9] but more often, even when setting recapitulated lines, Shepherd avoided a literal musical return. A section might refer back momentarily to the beginning but continue differently.[10] Sometimes later sections resemble an interior section rather than the first.[11] In several songs the sense of return is achieved not in the vocal part but in accompaniment interludes,[12] or introduction and coda frames,[13] while the vocal part itself is through-composed. In at least one, *Spinning Song* (1949),* the accompaniment goes through a process of retransition,[14] creating a strong desire for a return, but at the point where the recapitulation is expected the song continues again in through-composed manner.[15] In *Spring Duet* (1942)* and *Psalm XLII* (1944) we find ternary forms that expand into through-composed final sections. Strophic forms, on the other hand, are very rare; I know of only two works that repeat music for more than one stanza of text.[16]

A perplexing problem in Shepherd's music in general, and in his songs in particular, is the matter of definitive versions. In works for which two or more copies are left, differences among them are the rule. In fact, when I catalogued the manuscripts after his death I found some songs existing in half a dozen or more variants. He did not normally change the idea or shape of the music, but merely the finish. He meddled with the texture, changed the key, rewrote an accompaniment, or rebarred a phrase. *Second Sonata* and *Triptych* were overhauled in this manner when second printings were needed. This tendency would seem natural if he simply felt that his intentions had not been realized; but he seemed unable to leave alone even works that had received several successful performances and would normally be considered finished. Though his friends chided him about it, he often picked the music apart, searching, it seemed, for some necessary improvement.

Songs—his own and those of others—occupied a special place close to Shepherd's heart. He loved the poetry that he set, and he took pains to set it well. His thirty or more songs contain his most intimate music and show in a particularly clear light some of the most admirable facets of his talent.

ARTISTIC MATURITY AND RETIREMENT

CHAPTER 6

During the thirties and forties Shepherd's life was tranquil as he lived, taught, and composed in Cleveland. For some years he presented chamber music concerts on the Cleveland radio. *Horizons, Second Sonata, Triptych,* and the Violin Sonata were being heard in ever-widening circles. *Horizons,* which had been taken to Europe in 1932 by Fabien Sevitsky, narrowly missed a performance in London through a mixup in the delivery of the parts. The E Minor String Quartet (No. 1), *The Song of the Pilgrims,* and the Piano Quintet also received numerous performances, furthering his reputation as one of the most able if not adventurous of American composers. The Symphony No. 2, performed by the Cleveland and Boston orchestras in 1940, failed to win its foothold in the repertoire, however, an experience that left him curiously hesitant over his adequacy in this mode of expression. Nine years later he wrote to Newman:

> And what can I say about the Symphony No. 2? Remembering *your* own labors in its behalf; remembering the strenuous preparation for the Cleveland performances,[1] remembering too the Boston performances[2] and the thorough panning that it received! The work represents a big question mark with me; wondering if in the hands of Szell or someone equally competent the thing might not be worth reviving. Or, does it indicate that I have not made the grade towards self-sufficient symphonic utterance? It might be so. There are works in the chamber-music list that seem to come closer, and less dependent upon extraneous ideas. Even so, for better or worse, all my stuff must be considered objectively, in one category or another.[3]

Also, in 1937 Shepherd was awarded an honorary doctorate from Western Reserve University, and in 1941 he was elected to membership in the National Institute of Arts and Letters.

He was now devoting significant time to composition, for he completed more works in 1941 than in any other year. All are one-movement pieces of moderate dimensions, continuing the trend toward small forms that had begun in the thirties. That this was a conscious redirection of his efforts is confirmed by letters of Percy Goetschius, to whom Shepherd had written of his intention to practice more extensively in small forms. He did not give up large forms: *Overture Hilaritas* (1942) for concert band, Third String Quartet (1944), the *Fantasy Overture on Down East Spirituals* (1946), *Variations on an Original Theme* for orchestra, and the Violin Concerto (1946) were all composed between 1941 and 1952. After 1951 the number of completed works declined sharply.

Early in 1943 Artur Rodzinski, then conductor of the Cleveland Orchestra, was called to the podium of the New York Philharmonic-Symphony Orchestra. The move, apparently unexpected, led some of the directors of the Cleveland Orchestra to advocate relying for a time on guest conductors, from among whom Rodzinski's successor could be chosen. Others argued that a season under temporary leadership would not only be detrimental to the orchestra, but would seriously increase the difficulty of securing adequate financial support for the new season. Many conductors applied for the post, and it seems that for a time there was a pulling and hauling among interested parties as candidates and patrons maneuvered for advantage.

Herbert Elwell, Deems Taylor, and Arthur Shepherd proposed that an American be selected. Taylor, intermission commentator for the radio broadcasts of the New York Philharmonic-Symphony Orchestra, brought the matter to the attention of the entire country. Elwell, critic for the Cleveland *Plain Dealer,* spoke out against the discrimination which had kept American conductors out of good orchestras for seventy-five years. Shepherd wrote to newspaper editors, board members, and other influential persons, explaining that American culture must eventually and rightly depend upon American artists. He attempted to counter the widespread feeling that Europeans, by reason of environment and training, are more musical than the offspring of our younger, different culture. A "different" culture requires its own art. His wife recalled:

> We talked too about the need for American conductors; because Arturus believed there are interpretations of music that can be realized only by persons of our culture.[4]

Shepherd denounced the widespread mistrust in the talents of American musicians. He confidently credited them, as a body, with abilities equal to any musical task. He pleaded for significant opportunities for American conductors on the grounds that all they required to develop their skills to the fullest was the experience of conducting good orchestras. He felt that if this opportunity were denied now in Cleveland, the American conductor would remain in limbo for at least another ten years.

The matter generated some heat in Cleveland's musical circles. Thoughtful replies to Shepherd's letters developed a variety of positions. Some continued to stress the inherent advantages of the European cultural matrix in the development of musical talent. Most, however, suppressed the issue of foreign birth, answering that Shepherd was out of bounds, chauvinistic, merely advocating a type of musical nationalism. The only valid consideration, they argued, was to obtain the best available man, to decide the question purely on the basis of musical competence. Rodzinski, interviewed by columnist William F. McDermott of the Cleveland *Plain Dealer,* spoke of his concern and "agitation" over what he considered to be a conscious effort, possibly organized, to set Americans against one another. In time of war, he said, we should especially heed our ideals, unite in our devotion to America's traditional concern for the individual's rights, and guard against any tendency to discriminate against foreign-born citizens.

Elwell and Shepherd countered that historically the discrimination had been the other way round. They pointed out that Rodzinski himelf, Leopold Stokowski, and other foreign-born conductors had learned their art by conducting American orchestras. They contended that natives had been deprived of the opportunities essential to mastery of this craft. Elwell denied distinguishing between Americans on the matter of their birth. He was not opposed to obtaining the best man. He merely asserted that qualified persons were not receiving the consideration due them, and he wanted equal opportunity. Shepherd, sticking to his long-range viewpoint, maintained that American society has an obligation to provide native-born musicians with the means of attaining the fruition of their talent. He championed Albert Stoessel, composer, conductor, and teacher at the Juilliard Graduate School in New York and an excellent all-around musician with wide experience in conducting. Stoessel, he felt, possessed an ideal combination of talents for the appointment in Cleveland. There is still in Shepherd's files a poignant letter in which Stoessel expresses his disappointment at the final outcome and appreciation for Shepherd's efforts in his behalf. When the decision had been reached in favor of Erich Leinsdorf, Deems Taylor sent a note dated April 6, 1943, to Shepherd:

> My dear Arthur Shepherd;
> Well, we tried.
> Sincerely yours,
> Deems Taylor

It is interesting to reflect how close Shepherd came on this occasion to the Americanism espoused by Farwell and the Wa-Wan Society, a philosophy that in 1909 he had not been able fully to accept. As Farwell had been, Shepherd had come to be ahead of his time. And as Farwell had given up after the Wa-Wan effort, this was Shepherd's last active campaign in behalf of Americanism in music.

On October 29, 1943, Percy Goetschius died. Asked to write a memorial article for the *Musical Quarterly,* Shepherd was soon corresponding with Goetschius's family, friends, and former students to collect information, anecdotes, testimonials, and memories. His purpose was to describe Goetschius as he appeared to students and colleagues, to humanize the lofty and formidable impression given by his *Applied Counterpoint* and *The Larger Forms of Musical Composition.* After a brief sketch of Goetschius's student days and his term as "Royal Württemberg Professor of Music" in Stuttgart, punctuated by anecdotes of his visits to Liszt and Brahms, he described Goetschius's activities at the New England Conservatory: his beautiful pianism, his elegant diction in the classroom, and above all his infectious enthusiasm for music. Goetschius's letters filled out the account:

Percy Goetschius

> Again you will find a few pencil marks; do not be annoyed; that is my life-work, you know, and I simply cannot help it. As angel I shall be kodaked with a blue pencil in my hand and a profoundly reflective countenance.[5]

The New York period of Goetschius's career provided the opportunity for short, critical evaluations of his several influential textbooks. Shepherd pointed out both their strengths and weaknesses: the acute artistic perception on which they rest and their excellent organization as well as the masses of minutiae that obscure the general principles they illustrate and a near-myopic concentration upon the period from Bach to Brahms. Strictly speaking, Goetschius was not a theorist—certainly not in the sense that Jean-Philippe Rameau and Paul Hindemith are theorists.

> There never could be a question, however, as to his authoritative gifts as a pedagogue of the first order. He was at his best seated at the piano, expounding, exhorting, underlining, and elucidating, never missing a trick in exposing each and every device of harmony, counterpoint, or structural syntax.[6]

The *Musical Quarterly* article is sympathetic and understanding, devoted to recording Goetschius's human qualities. The treatment was appropriate, for in his chosen field Goetschius could express himself most ably.

These years saw the deaths of some of Shepherd's closest friends and supporters. His wife recalled the sadness of this period:

> And then Beryl[7] died, and Dud[8] died, and Al Brewster died, and we left the house on Richmond Road.[9] We moved to an apartment in town.[10] We left the "Congress Tree" in the country. We always called a certain great tree outside the windows the Congress Tree because the birds sat there on their migrations to talk things over. We left the bird bath that meant so much to us, and the little "Padre's garden" which lay outside the doors of Arturus's studio.[11] We left the Christmas trees which had been planted through the years, and had grown high as the apple trees. And we left the little peach tree which was fruiting for the first time. Peter[12] and I had planted the seed.
>
> We went to an apartment where there were people above and below us. There were no floods of light, nor air, nor sound, no insect hum at night, no fireplaces in or out. But Arturus had a studio down at the University in a lovely old house; this due to the courtesy and consideration of Dr. Seymour,[13] who had been a student at Western Reserve earlier, and was in charge of the . . . medical buildings of the University at this time.
>
> We took to the parks. We used to go out day after day to the various parks that surround Cleveland. We learned to be very grateful for the vision of those who had made this green circle possible. We took charcoal and chops and cheese and wine, and so found the air, and the light, and the sounds of the earth that we were missing . . . and it was along in here that the deafness became a very, very present trouble. Sometimes in his efforts to hear the baseball game over the radio at the apartment, he turned the machine up so high that it bothered others. . . .[14]

But though his life after 1940 appears routine and calm, Shepherd's activities were many. He was composing at a quick pace. From his classroom there remain masses of notes, and his moderate prominence as an educator brought requests for lectures and articles for professional organizations and meetings. He worked continually to strengthen the music department of the university. One of his achievements in this direction was to give Manfred Bukofzer his first position in the United States as Lecturer in Music at Western Reserve University in 1940–41.[15] By the time Shepherd retired in 1950 at the age of seventy he had built the undergraduate and graduate curricula into a department of vitality and energy. In the words of a colleague:

> Surely the development of the Division of Music was his work, and even though each of us was working in a separate department we all found our standards and our artistic leadership in him.[16]

The conclusion of a quarter-century of service to the university prompted a series of occasions and attentions in his honor, for which Shepherd was grateful, although at times embarrassed. "I am blushing all over the place because of the Sturm und Drang occasioned by my superannuation."[17] Contemplation of retirement left him with a sense of insecurity and concern for the future, and his relief was evident when arrangements for the next year were consummated:

> Next Sunday I shall be off to Boston and Cambridge to make a Commencement address at Longy School. M[elville] Smith threw out a life line by way of an invitation to teach there next season, so I grabbed it! I like the prospect.[18]

Mrs. Shepherd relates that on his return he glowed over that year of warm fellowship and endless musical talk with his old friend as one of his richest experiences. Another symptom of emotional stress occasioned by his retirement was a lapse in creative work:

> The turn of this particular "mile post" is fraught with so many unpredictable problems and prospects that I have a queer feeling of disorientation. I can only wish that the state of mind did not affect my creative efforts.[19]

Several of his works were performed in recognition of his retirement. George Szell and the Cleveland Orchestra gave a magnificent reading of *Overture to a Drama* at the first concert in December 1949, a revival that for a while generated new enthusiasm for this effective work.[20] Szell also tendered a commission for a new orchestral work, *Variations on an Original Theme,* which received its first performances on April 9 and 11, 1953. *Second Sonata* was played by Beryl Rubinstein for the Music Teachers National Association at its December 1949 meetings, and on January 8, 1950, a program of chamber music included the *Sonata for Pianoforte and Violin, Triptych,* and the *Quartet for Strings in E Minor.* In May the *Quintet for Pianoforte and Strings* was played as the final work in a festival of contemporary music at the Cleveland Museum of Art. *Triptych* was accorded a place in a similar festival at Columbia University. In describing the New York performance Shepherd wrote to Newman:

> Thanks for sending me the Downes[21] clipping. I was present at the performance and was pleased with the outcome. The audience reaction to my music was very warm and the performance first class, the best ever for this piece.[22]

Shepherd's retirement was also noted in the pages of *The Musical Quarterly.*[23] Written by William S. Newman, former student and close friend, this article is the best ready source on Shepherd's life and works. It details briefly, accurately, and with admirable thoroughness the main facts of the composer's life. Newman also devoted considerable attention to technical and stylistic discussions of his music. He outlined the various types and forms with which Shepherd worked and pointed out the characteristics by which his music is recognized.

By reason of his study with and admiration for Arthur Shepherd, Newman was the logical choice for this task. Shepherd in turn recognized the importance and honor it represented for them both. Responding to a questionnaire, he disclosed many facts and opinions that enabled Newman to write clearly and with insight. Bundles of manuscripts and published works were sent for Newman to peruse, and the accompanying letters testify further to the emotional turmoil of the experience:

> Assembling the material is for me a devastatingly self-revealing business, but may in some unpredictable way, be of considerable worth.[24]

He described the experience of looking through forgotten or by now unfamiliar compositions. In the light of perspective he admitted that despite many interesting details he disliked the "flavor" of some of the old works. Lacking good performances, he could no longer judge them. Yet the project forced him to judge not only his accomplishments but his beliefs, motivations, and aspirations; it became in effect a personal evaluation of his life and works. Looking at himself as objectively as possible as a complete and finished artist was both difficult and painful. The remembrance of high goals and hard work, the realization that in all likelihood greatness had eluded him, and the knowledge that too little time and energy remained for further major efforts depressed him. Yet the experience seemed to widen his perspective and enabled him to carry on in his remaining years with dignity, continued production, and increased insight and perception. When the article appeared he wrote Newman:

> I have written notes of appreciation to Lang and Broder.[25] *Yours* ought to have come first! But *adequate* appreciation in your direction is hard to express.[26]

It was about this time that a recording of Shepherd's piano music was made, one that he never heard in its final form as a phonodisc.[27] Mrs. Shepherd recounts this story:

> Along in the forties came some new people into our lives who were exceedingly important to him. One was Honoré Gilbeau, an artist who also is a musician. She

and Vivien Slater, who later made the record of Arturus's piano music, and Herbert Pasch, Jerry Gross,[28] and Charles Loeser, of the medical school, studied with Arturus, and they became rare companions because they were fond of him and understood him and appreciated him. . . . Later Arturus worked with Vivien Slater intensively on a recording of his piano works. There were innumerable difficulties with the people who were going to produce the record, and as a consequence it was not published during his lifetime. . . . I think it captures the spirit of Arthur Shepherd in the most accurate possible fashion. He loved tone for its own sake. He loved lyricism, and these piano pieces seem to me to emphasize these particular characteristics.

There was another record made after his death.[29] This was the recording of the songs sung by Marie Kraft. Both these records were financed by friends. The Slater record in particular owes a great deal to the efforts of Klaus Roy, who is the program annotator of the Cleveland Orchestra. . . . He came to Cleveland after Arturus died, but it was really through his putting together of parts that Vivien Slater's record has finally come into publication.[30]

Following his retirement and his year at the Longy School in Cambridge Shepherd's life was spent in composition, music study, reading, and preparations for performances, recordings, and publications of his music. His partial deafness handicapped him but he remained active and progressed in his art. As opportunities arose he conducted, lectured, wrote, or taught occasional classes. Composing was now slow, sometimes painfully so; but the works written during his retirement are among his finest. In connection with all these activities and to acknowledge various honors that came to him, he traveled both to the East and West coasts, making new acquaintances, renewing old friendships, and radiating not only insights drawn from his remarkable musical sensitivity and long experience but also the sincerity, cheer, and goodwill for which he was admired.

One of his great satisfactions at this time was to be able to purchase a house. The Shepherds had never owned their own home, and life in the Lennox Road apartment had seemed very confined after the freedom and quiet of the Richmond Road house. Mrs. Shepherd tells of this decision:

One day when the air was so still, and one felt the noise of the living beings in this apartment intensively, I said, "I know a place where the wind blows." It was the little hill adjoining the house we now occupy which you know.

Arturus said, "Well, why haven't we looked at this house?" because we had been looking for a house we might buy.

And I said, "The living room isn't big enough for your piano."

. . . "Well, if I have to give up the studio at the University, we could put a small piano in that large bedroom upstairs and I would be content."[31]

It was during this period that I met Shepherd in Cleveland to look into the possibility of writing a dissertation on his life and works. I had trouble finding his studio—the music room of an otherwise unoccupied mansion near Western Reserve University—phoned him for directions, and found him waiting on the sidewalk before the house when I arrived. His appearance was distinguished; though rather small in stature, he gave the impression—as his good friend Edward G. Evans, Jr., who then headed the music department at the university, has noted—of being taller than he was. He wore both spectacles and a hearing aid. Though past seventy, he was energetic, positive, and confident. He was cordial toward my project, though it must then have seemed to him no more promising than several he had already endured. Our conversation on music in general and his own music in particular aroused in me an uncommon interest. It was my initial experience with the enthusiasm and communicative powers that have been remarked upon by so many of his students, and it was a good beginning.

I spent portions of three summers in Cleveland. During the first two I enjoyed a close fellowship with Shepherd, conversing frequently with him about music and about his life and experiences. His manuscripts, which were scattered casually if not haphazardly about the studio, obviously lay at the heart of the matter; these and much of his correspondence I collected, classified, and filed. Needing copies for study at home during the winter and hoping at the same time to preserve the music from possible loss through ruin of the manuscripts, I photographed most of those that Shepherd designated as definitive scores; this project was possibly the most significant single contribution of my Eastman dissertation. Unrestricted access to old letters and programs was of great help to me in writing Shepherd's biography, which received his approval in 1957 while he was visiting for a few days at my home in Claremont, California.

Shepherd's personal style and his manner of living and conversing were impressive. He was as aware of the activities of his contemporaries in music and the other arts and of the political and social problems of his day as he was of his own work. His opinions were individual and forceful, his insights into everyday life keen, and his interests diverse.

He relishes Little Abner and Damon Runyon, owns all we can get [about them]. A woman, now a great voice

Arthur Shepherd (standing) with his wife Grazella and their son Peter on vacation around 1940.

teacher, told me, "When I was seventeen he took *Science and Health* out of my hands and put *Leaves of Grass* into them. He has aways known and chosen the best as if by instinct." He loves Whitman still as you know. Recently he has enjoyed enormously the Sitwell books and especially Edith Sitwell's poems. He has written a setting for one—it will be used in the January program of the Fine Arts series.[32]

The Shepherds took great pleasure in their travels, both before and after his retirement.

We went to see Mr. Goetschius, because Arturus loved him. We went to California where we were the guests of the Henry Eichheims in Santa Barbara in a magic time. We went to Lausanne, Switzerland, where Arturus played in a big musical event with André de Ribaupierre, a native of Switzerland and a former teacher at the Institute of Music. . . . We went to London and to Scotland. . . . We summered twice in New England and twice in Florida; one summer on Canandaigua Lake, New York. We made at least four trips by car across to Utah. I think we enjoyed every minute of it because both of us loved the expanse of . . . the earth and the sky, and the wonder of Yellowstone, the wonder of the Snake River, the wonder of the beauty of that great Great Basin. As I look back I can see we lived it up—and I'm glad we did![33]

Shepherd loved activity. In his younger days he had played some baseball, and in his later years he still enjoyed attending a Cleveland Indians game on a summer afternoon.

He loved tennis. He loved to walk. We were both sorry in the last ten years that we had never played cards nor played games. Some of this is my fault because I never had played to win, and you can't be a good player of games if you don't want to win. . . . [As to his] preferences in entertainment, he loved *Showboat,* and one of the happiest experiences toward the end was seeing *My Fair Lady.* His daughter-in-law had gotten a copy of it for him to read before he went, and his delight in the whole thing was something to remember forever. He believed . . . that there was a peculiar American twist in this nature of musical performance.[34]

And he loved to talk:

Through all our lives there was endless, endless talk. Elmer Davis[35] was as present in our talks as if he had been there in person. In conversation too, as if present in body, was Albert Schweitzer, always—and of course Brahms, Beethoven, and Bach, Vincent d'Indy, William Blake. And a fascinating thing comes back to me to indicate how the conversation, the words that were used, came to be part of the whole household. . . . We used to make salad at the table, and Arturus always mixed it. One night it didn't turn out very well and Peter, then a little boy, said, "Well, it lacks form!" . . . Among the other people that were talked about all the time was Gertrude Stein. And I remember endless references to *The Hound of Heaven* by Francis Thompson. We talked through the years about every conceivable thing, and I remember that the Sunday before Arturus went to the hospital at the end we sat down at the breakfast table at nine and left it at one.[36]

His death, on January 12, 1958, was unexpected, the result of unforeseen complications that arose during a routine surgical operation. He died, as he had lived, in the middle of things; he had carried an unfinished song and notes for some lectures to the hospital to occupy him during his convalescence. The tragedy of his passing was heightened by everyone's expectation that he had many years yet before him, for he was descended from a family of long-lived people. But the anticipated happiness of the years ahead probably depended upon his productivity, and in one sense he was relieved of the possibility of a greater tragedy. The main concerns that necessarily arose with advancing age were his encroaching deafness, the possible drying-up of springs of musical inspiration, and consequent musical inactivity. For him I think a life without music would have been irremediably impoverished. His body is buried in the family plot in the Salt Lake City Cemetery.

It seems fitting at this point to say a few words regarding Arthur Shepherd's religion. He was born, raised, and first married in the Mormon Church, but sometime between the first and second marriages he left the church for reasons that I do not know. My own conversations with him did not explore these matters fully. My memory is that he was deeply conscious of a Supreme Being but distrustful of man's collective and organized dogmas concerning Him.

In 1958 Shepherd's library—including musical manuscripts, teaching notes, his collection of programs, and other personalia—was presented to the Freiberger Library of Western Reserve University by his wife for use by musicians and scholars. In 1973 it was transferred to the Marriott Library of Fine Arts of the University of Utah in Salt Lake City. The manuscript collection is in good order and, fortunately, is virtually complete.[37] Only a few scores are missing, and the locations of some of these are known. Many works exist in several scores or copies, among which there are often slight differences. In many cases a comparison of the copies has made it possible to decide upon the probable order of the various versions of a work. In Appendix A I have explained the importance of collating these materials before publication, important performances, or recordings are undertaken. Their presence and availability in one place makes the task both possible and pleasant.

In this book will be found much of Arthur Shepherd's curious and beautiful music. It will show that he was a traditional composer, out of step with the newest expressions of his time. While Schoenberg turned toward the emancipation of dissonance and pantonality Shepherd adhered to the primacy of consonance and tonality—yet his methods of creating a "key" and his uses of all the intervals are fresh and individual.

Where Varèse and Ives juxtaposed or combined Impressionistic and Expressionistic masses Shepherd held to Beethovenian—Apollonian—notions of form and texture, based on melodic thematic material, key relationships, and thoroughly tested methods of exposition, contrast, variation, and development. And yet his forms are, in their way, unique—they are not molded by patterns, but issue out of an unfettered intercourse between those forces.

Despite admiration for Stravinsky and Bartók he did not follow them (as they had followed Monteverdi) into newer realms of rhythmic and dissonant passion. Like Fauré and Loeffler he uttered a lyric speech which called on music for gentler, more delicate purposes—yet his narrower expressive territory is as filled with nuance and as complex in interior relationships as that of those eminent pioneers. Among the leaders of his day he seems to have had the closest rapport with Hindemith, possibly because his books explained clearly the traditional roots of his music, yet Shepherd's sound is wholly his own.

Shepherd was perhaps more desirous than they of communicating with his immediate audience and of causing a reaction in it. He wanted his music to be logical, ingenious, and craftworthy, but also expressive, attractive, and somehow representative of the aspirations of its time and place. However, his time and place—an American university wrapped up as much in the past as in the present—quite likely limited his vision, in contrast to the theatrical and concert milieu of Stravinsky and Bartók or the interior and philosophical vistas of Ives and Schoenberg. Shepherd wanted his music to last, but I do not think he wrote for the future.

It is easy to prove that Shepherd did not make use of important techniques that make some music "contemporary," but this was because those developments did not measure up to *his* requirements. What he wrote speaks eloquently to many of what he believed, and these beliefs still hold an appeal for many. His great ability and high ideals imparted to his work an interest, an honesty and integrity, a quality, and a beauty that may be recognized and appreciated in the future, when there is less anxiety over being in tune with the times and when the terrific cross-currents that have divided one decade from another appear only as ripples in the mainstream of the art.

Shepherd's approach to art and life was optimistic and joyful, but also deeply serious and directed by lofty ideals. His music was of necessity art music. He had no illusions as to his importance in the developmental stream of things. Rather, he looked confidently for the coming genius—as for a messiah—who would synthesize the multitudinous trends of the present into the powerful expressions within the capabilities of contemporary music. Yet he knew his own power; he had seen his music sway audiences. And he was confident that, through talent and hard work, he had created a beautiful and durable part of the great edifice being constructed by composers past, present, and future.

With what was given him he did all that any man can do: he realized his talent.

PART TWO:

THE BOSTON STYLE: THE MUSIC TO ABOUT 1923

CHAPTER 7

A few works from Shepherd's student days have survived and one, *Romanza for the Pianoforte,* was published in an 1896 issue of the *Quarterly* of the New England Conservatory of Music. It is a small ternary form, *Andante moderato* in C major, similar to the *Songs without Words* of Mendelssohn but with perhaps even slightly more of the salon atmosphere than those pleasant pieces. If its style is light, it possesses nevertheless that close agreement between intent and technique that marks the work of a real composer. The only evidence of the exuberance and posing that might be expected of a lad of fifteen is a propensity to exaggerate the texture and dynamic range out of proportion with the length of the piece, and use epic utterance for a small verse form. The score is spotted with the crescendos and decrescendos, accelerandos and ritards, dramatic leaps, octave textures, and assorted accents, slurs, and expressives that are marks of its time. In spite of this, one detects a feeling for form and drama in its structure, in the shaping and occasional extension of phrases, in the use of modulation and chromatic harmony to enhance contrasts and climax, and in the expert composition of the retransition and coda. We cannot know how much its craftsmanship reflects the steady hand of Percy Goetschius, whose textbook, *The Homophonic Forms of Musical Composition,* had been published just five years previously. Reports of Goetschius's instruction, however, suggest that he relied not so much on form patterns as on form principles, gained from close analysis of works by the masters. I think we can accept the *Romanza* as Arthur's piece and thus an indication of the natural quality of the talent with which we are dealing. Later works also indicate that his genius, though subject to intellectual control, was more akin in the spontaneity of its conception to Schubert than Beethoven.

From about 1900 to 1923 Shepherd relied primarily on traditional methods of composition. His sonorities were tertian, his textures lush and sensuous. His music was typical of the better-equipped American composers of the time, tailored to European patterns and following one or another of the contemporary musical fashions. If he was more active than some of his academic colleagues in his concern for American music, he did join them in a general healthy respect for the musical traditions of the old countries. For a few years after 1900 his harmony was adventurous enough to be thought advanced—at least this was the opinion maintained in an account of his work in *The Art of Music,* an encyclopedia published in 1915. Probably written by Arthur Farwell, who served as an editor for the volume on American music, the article reads in part:

> One of the most keenly individualized of American composers, and one of the most daring and original in the employment of ultra-modern resource, is Arthur Shepherd, formerly of Salt Lake City and at present connected with the New England Conservatory of Music in Boston, Mass. His work, as a whole, is almost unique in American music in the completeness of its departure from the styles of any individual composers who may earlier have stimulated or influenced him. The dominating factor in his work, almost from the beginning, has been the will to express himself in a certain manner, wholly his own. . . . His harmony would make any other German than a radical Strauss enthusiast shrink with horror, so sweeping and so subversive of the usual order are its departures from the accepted scheme, while, on the other hand, it can be said to be very little suggestive of the characteristic quality of the modern French

school. Especially it eschews the luscious and velvety harmonic surface of Debussy. In both melody and harmony the saccharine—even the merely sweet—the sensuous and the languorous, Shepherd dethrones with the sedulous intolerance of a Pfitzner and, like that composer, exalts in its place a clear and luminous spiritual beauty. Other wise he works in that art, in chords that bite and grip, and rises often to a great nobility of conception and expression.[1]

Farwell's description, now over sixty years old, raises before us totally different images from those he intended. From our vantage the harmony of Shepherd's early music is more closely related to the common practice than independent of it.[2] It is rooted in the interlaced concepts of the seven-toned diatonic scale with subsidiary chromaticism, the construction of chords by thirds, the phenomenon of nonharmonic tones, and the primacy of key. Anyone who cares to test Shepherd's prowess in wholly traditional harmony and counterpoint need only read his C-sharp Minor Fugue* for piano (1920), which, if indistinguishable from hundreds of other "school fugues," yet shows in the most convincing way (perhaps its real purpose) his understanding and mastery of this venerable technique, this standard by which academic work was judged in his time.

Other works, many earlier than the fugue, illustrate his ability to use traditional materials in more original and independent ways. A little anthem for women's chorus, *He Came All So Still** (published in 1915, but available here in a later arrangement for solo voice and piano) reveals an exquisite treatment of the simplest harmonic materials of the traditional style. It illustrates more effectively than the somewhat pretentious fugue the imagination and ingenuity that characteristically enhance Shepherd's works. Comparing the song with textbook maxims, one notices first a tendency to freshness in the harmonizations of the cadences, and second, an overall bias toward harmony favoring the flat side of the key. See for example the accidentals in the melody (all but one are diatonically used) and the harmonic shift toward six flats at "Mother and maiden . . .".

Examples of typical early works include the songs *Sun Down* (1909),* *Sunday up the River* (1912),* and *The Gentle Lady* (c.1916).* Shepherd was of the opinion that this manuscript of *Sun Down* is in Arthur Farwell's hand. As references to the singing lark pervade the poem, so has Shepherd utilized a little twittering motive in the accompaniment. Most of the harmony is typical, but on page 3 ("And the darkening air . . .") the succession of chords moves under the influence of ostinato and linear melodic forces more than under that of traditional root movement. The sudden shift from an F minor to an E minor triad that sets "the great gift of sleep" is a noteworthy touch. I find it fascinating to compare this passage with the elaborate harmonic preparation of the final word "death," which is richly laden with flattened notes in B major—C-natural, A-natural, G-natural—ever pressing downwards to the cadence, until a rising dominant triad suddenly regains the full brilliance of B major, matching the sense of fulfillment and peace that this poem conveys about one's passing.

If one hears the bird songs and the affective harmonies of *Sun Down* as examples of text painting, he will not be surprised by the accompaniment of *Sunday up the River.* Shepherd's command of sonority is set to the creation of pianistic evocations of church bells diffused throughout the text. We hear artistic equivalents of the strike and hum tones of large bells and the pealing of carillons. The final phrase, essentially plagal in its goal, again explores flat-side alterations, this time very close to pure Dorian harmony. In both these songs, as well as in *The Gentle Lady,* Shepherd achieved some of the individuality he sought through imaginative cadences.

The Gentle Lady, dedicated to his sister Josephine, was Shepherd's contribution to *The Art of Music* (the editors included a work by each composer whom they discussed). At first glance it is a simple and straightforward song in A major. Closer inspection reveals a curious twist in the tonality, a stressing of the subdominant because of a tendency in the melodic phrases to move from or toward prominently placed D-naturals (both high and low). But the temptation to invoke D Lydian to satisfy analysis is scuttled by the ending, unmistakably centered on A. Furthermore, our concept of modal harmony implies a more diatonic idiom than is heard here. Shepherd swamped the mode in a rich, chromatically influenced harmony similar to that of the *Overture to a Drama.* Only a weak modal coloration remains, again a hint of things to be.

The text is set in a rhythmic and melodic garb nicely related to the syllabification, declamation, prosody, and sense of the words. The last verse especially ("So simple sweet . . .") is a marvel of text setting. One long phrase, it rises gradually in successive waves to its highest note. At the end ("To tunes the laughing bells have chimed.") the accompaniment delicately evokes the bells by the use of parallel sonorities (clangs) together with the distinctive symbols for harmonics (°), borrowed from string notation, that occur from time to time in Shepherd's piano notation.[3] For its time *The Gentle*

Lady is a forward-looking American song of high imagination and subtle workmanship. Though I search it in vain for "ultra-modern" resources, I admit its individuality. I can readily agree with *The Art of Music* that Shepherd in this song demonstrated a desire "to express himself in a certain manner, wholly his own."

In this period Shepherd worked in the seven-tone diatonic scale with subsidiary chromatic tones rather than in a tonal scale of twelve nearly equal degrees.[4] Of this scale there are twelve tonics and a number of forms (major, minor, and the various modes)—altogether an inexhaustible storehouse of materials. The melodies of the songs *Sun Down, Sunday up the River,* and *The Gentle Lady* illustrate this point. In each many chromatic alterations appear, but none uses chromaticism in the form of the alteration of a diatonic note. Rather, accidentals accrue from the momentary adoption of another scale. An especially apt example occurs in *Sun Down,* page 4: "Night with her train of stars, and her great gift of sleep."

These melodies are lyrical and expressive, for Shepherd a basic type. In later instrumental works we shall see that he was also capable of active, disjunct, and wide-ranging melodic utterance. Much of his attention was devoted to the discovery of melodies whose expressive content tallied closely with the mood of the text he was setting or the dramatic effect that he required. He exercised similar care in fitting a melody to its medium, carefully exploiting the most effective ranges and tessituras of both instruments and voices. Customarily he reserved very high notes for climaxes. Instrumental melodies are more extended in their range than those composed for voices, and solos are more intricate than chorus or orchestral parts. The tonality of a melody is often established by stressing one tone of the tonic triad or an appoggiatura to such a tone. This stressing may be rhythmic in nature or may be accomplished by some sensitive melodic factor in the construction of the phrase that makes of the tone a beginning, ending, or climax point. From these remarks it will be seen that his melodic thought is traditional. His interest in melody lay in its ability to delight and satisfy. He was disinterested in lines that were distorted or grotesque, or even in the super-expressive style of the early Schoenberg.[5]

Rhythmically, the most significant trend over the years was a gradual liberation of Shepherd's melodic rhythm from the regularity of metrical pulse. He achieved this flexibility by an increase in syncopation, a relative decrease in the number of phrases in which the rhythm agrees with the meter, and greater use of mixed (changing) meters.

Though it cannot be illustrated here, I must mention the harmonic language of the prize-winning cantata, *The City in the Sea,* which reveals an eclectic, if limited, absorption of the spirit of Impressionism as well as a fluency in the chromaticism and harmonic meandering of the late Romantic period. It is also here, so far as I am aware, that Shepherd approached closest to the dialect of Richard Wagner. But also, even at the very opening of the cantata, there appear modal tinges, harbingers of his later music; and in the long baritone solo that sets the more personal, inner stanzas of Bliss Carman's poem we hear the free chromatic and modulatory flux characteristic of German turn-of-the-century music. If *The City in the Sea* is heady with appoggiaturas, pedal tones and pedal chords, tall tertian dissonances, and the wide spacings so effective in the large Romantic orchestra, if it enjoys an occasional Franckian shifting of the chromaticism or occasionally an Impressionistic whole-tone measure, if it is eclectic in spirit, it is nevertheless a convincing and individual mixture of all these elements. If today any of Shepherd's music is brought to mind by the remarks of Farwell quoted earlier, it is surely the grand ebb and flow of sound that must have been heard in the Chicago performances of this cantata under Frederick Stock.

Many of these early works exhibit a youthful fire and enthusiasm that the later music does well to match, as might be seen in a comparison of the baritone solo of *The City in the Sea* with the tenor solo of the cantata *The Song of the Pilgrims* (1932). Of the latter Shepherd wrote:

> Now there is one passage that I am specially fond of: the Tenor solo *page 9* cadencing on p. 10 on the words "being happy," *then* on page 11 in the reproduction of the passage in the key of G. "And dwell in little houses lovable, etc." *then* cadencing again on the words "being happy"—in the original key of A flat.[6]

I find the earlier passage, that from *The City in the Sea,* to be vigorous, imaginative, full of the intensity of youth, and brimming with ideas. It seems hardly able to contain itself within its form, its orchestra, and its soloists and chorus. The pilgrims by contrast are cute. They sing anachronistic snatches of plainsong and modulate surprisingly about their "little houses lovable." It is all very subtle, ingenious, and contrived. Even more disturbing for me is to compare the treatment of death on page 11 of *The Song of the Pilgrims* with the passage in *Sun Down* mentioned earlier. Much, of course, was gained in technique, control, polish, and style in the nearly twenty years between the two cantatas; and the spontaneity and emotion of this early music is still present in some of the big works of the twenties, particularly *Triptych* (1925) and the Violin Sonata. After examining both the early and the late music, one will be in a position to decide for himself whether Shepherd's increased intellectual control over his music compensates sufficiently for the decline in his youthful ardor.

Of the larger works of the early period, the *Sonata for the Pianoforte*, Op. 4, and the *Overture to a Drama* (1919) are worthy of study. The sonata is flamboyant and youthful, made for virtuoso players and stocked with devices chosen for survival in early twentieth-century concert halls: emotional thematic material, colorful harmony, a wide range of moods, opportunity both for big sounds and delicate shadings, and long enough to impress. Goetschius considered the second movement sufficiently interesting to cite as a reference in the chapter on ground bass of his textbook, *The Larger Forms of Musical Composition.*

Overture to a Drama, composed four years after Farwell's critique, is a large, intense effort. We should expect nothing hasty in it, nothing less than Shepherd's best, written as it was after his tour of military duty and the shock of the domestic disaster that he suffered on his return from France. A mischievous spirit could scarcely have contrived experiences better calculated to force him into a serious and deep search for music commensurate with his state of mind. Lacking evidence that the overture was intended for a specific production, one assumes that it reflects the drama in his own life.

The opening theme is a long line which, by avoiding cadences, stretches out to fifteen measures, not without phrase delineation but certainly with little correspondence to customary relationships between antecedent and consequent phrases. The mood is energetic, the effect virile. Wild Straussian shapes are flung out by the horns, and the harmony is shot through with extensive chromatic deviations that eventually plunge back into a rock-solid A minor. The second subject, quiet, feminine, expressive, begins with a slowly arpeggiated seventh chord similar to Debussy's flaxen-haired maiden but harmonized by Romantic augmented sixths. Out of these materials Shepherd developed a sonata form of considerable scope, drama, and conviction.

The overture was performed a few times in Cleveland in the mid-twenties and thirties; then in 1949 a performance by George Szell and the Cleveland Orchestra electrified Shepherd. He wrote to William S. Newman:

> I have sent you a recent report concerning the (shall I say, surprising) success of this 30-year-old work. But, after all, what is 30 years by way of indication of surviving vitality in a musical composition? *And* maybe I should be a bit on guard concerning precise manifestations of interest, cordiality, etc. In some other environment this overture would undoubtedly be ticked off as thoroughly "dated" and romantically suffused with all the *old* cliches. But then again, there *may* be more to it. The instrumentation has always been admired. Szell was very complimentary and the most knowing of our musicians equally so. The upshot of this little flurry is that I have been cogitating anew about old questions relating to the *Communicative* vitality and expressive power inherent or latent in this or that composition; mine or the other fellow's.[7]

The City in the Sea was written in 1913. In this year of *The Rite of Spring* Shepherd's music was a swan-song of a passing way of art, destined for extinction in the ashes of the impending war. Despite Farwell's encomium there is nothing in Shepherd's early works to show that he was cognizant of the new ideas by which Stravinsky, Schoenberg, and Bartók were shaping the music of the future. Nor do we find any influence of Charles Ives, so near physically to Shepherd's Boston yet artistically so far ahead of his time. Like Farwell and Gilbert, Shepherd too had been looking the wrong way.

A case for Shepherd's music cannot be made for its innovative qualities, but rather for his expression of himself "in a certain manner wholly his own." His work possesses timeless expressive and musical values common to all good music. Now that the artistic turmoil of the days in which he wrote has settled into perspective and the innovators and their significant accomplishments have been sorted out, a second look at his music might be not only pleasurable but illuminating of a type of quiet beauty too easily overlooked.

THE CLEVELAND STYLE: THE TWENTIES TO 1958

CHAPTER 8

HARMONY AND RHYTHM

The influence of the modes on Shepherd's music was both known to him and noted by others. In writing of this influence I shall use the terms Dorian, Phrygian, Lydian, Mixolydian, and Aeolian, since Shepherd also used them. Because they are sometimes called ecclesiastical modes, it is worth mentioning that the influences I am describing reside in the scales themselves, not in any churchly atmosphere that they might connote.[1] If anything, Shepherd's music veers closer to English and Irish folk songs, where these modes are also found, than to the Gregorian melodies. The modes provided a melodic freshness and harmonic piquancy that he prized; but, more important, they enabled him to retain the tonal system that was for him essential. From some of his earliest music to the latest works we can trace his obvious delight in modal effects—sometimes in isolation and occasionally in sections of relatively concentrated modality, either pure, mixed with other modes, or affected by chromatic alteration and modulation.

Shepherd used modal notes both melodically and harmonically,[2] and he heightened their effect by treating them freely rather than resolving the strong tendencies they acquire when introduced into our major-minor system. Thus in *Reverie* (1932),* where all forms of the minor scale appear, he freely skips from sharp 6, or steps down to 5 (rather than resolve it to sharp 7). Thus *Reverie* is for me a basically Dorian conception. One also encounters mixed modes, such as the major scale with sharp 4 and flat 7, major with flat 6 and flat 7, minor with flat 2 and sharp 6, or minor with flat 6 and sharp 4. It is interesting that the first three of these mixed modes can also be described as modal forms of the melodic minor scale. The Phrygian mode is particularly prone to combinations of this sort.

All of these scales will be found in melodic snatches of a phrase or longer; the Dorian, Lydian, and Mixolydian are favored for longer melodies. Harmonically, the Dorian is rarer than the others. Shepherd did not explore the harmonic or melodic possibilities of modal writing over the long stretches of a form; hence his modality is seldom pure. Nevertheless, the references given in the footnotes include some of the longest and most consistent modal passages known to me, and through these one can judge for himself the relative modal purity of Shepherd's music.[3]

Shepherd used all the triads and sevenths, along with many higher tertian dissonances (ninths, elevenths, thirteenths) of the common practice.[4] Many of these also appear with added tones: seconds, fourths, sixths, minor thirds (to chords with major thirds).[5] He also added one or two dissonant notes (if two they are a perfect fourth or fifth) in the bass of triads or sevenths. Often, of course, dissonances in the bass are pedal tones, but many form legitimate independent chords. The Violin Sonata and *Triptych* are rich in them.[6]

In a technique employing such common harmonic materials one would expect to find the normal complement of nonharmonic tones. Passing and neighbor (auxiliary) tones are very common; appoggiaturas, escape tones (échappée), and anticipations are normal. Even that twentieth-century casualty, the suspension, is heard.[7] Pedal tones are favorites, especially when considered along with their cousins, stressed but discontinuous bass tones and ostinatos.[8]

More interesting are passages in which Shepherd carried the nonharmonic concept somewhat beyond the common practice. Here and there a melody is so laden with nonharmonic tones that it tends to separate from the harmony. One instance in *Lento Amabile* (1938) will be discussed later, but see also *In Modo Ostinato* (1945), meas. 8–10. Contrary to the melodic habits of Shepherd's earlier works, this technique emphasizes altered nonharmonic tones, frequently without resolution, at points of melodic stress, arrival, or climax.[9]

If these materials—the chords and nonharmonic tones—are largely traditional, what of their connections and progressions? Root movement analysis is not as enlightening as one might suppose. The presence and importance of rooted sonorities is undeniable, but the difficulty of determining the exact root of some complex chords, the influence of counterpoint and of certain contemporary sonorities, and the extended tonality of his early, formative years combine to weaken the ability of classic root movement theory to explain Shepherd's harmony. We search in vain for the patterns of fifth, second, and third root relations so significant in Baroque and Classic music. I shall not postulate, therefore, any general principles of harmonic progression according to root movement; rather, we shall look at specific, typical cases.

Shepherd sometimes did write in a harmonic style close to the common practice; examples of this style from early works have been discussed in Chapter 7. In the music now under consideration these passages normally manifest unusual points of resolution or emphasis that, despite the conventionality of the basic chordal motion, save his harmony from any hint of the choirloft. As an example the reader is referred to *Souvenir* (1945),* wherein root movement harmony is much in evidence, but where also the passage that achieves the final cadence chord, meas. 19–24, is admirably individual and imaginative.[10]

Particularly interesting progressions will be heard in passages where Shepherd has harmonized a familiar tune or reharmonized an earlier version of a theme. In "Canyons" (the last movement of *Horizons*, full score, p. 148 at letter O (see accompanying piano reduction of score), Shepherd set a hymn with quite modal harmonies. The inner parts move along melodic and motivic lines of their own, and the bass characteristically faults one's expectations at the cadences through deceptive movements or early arrival at a cadence tone.[11]

Horizons, "Canyons," page 148 ff at "O."[12]

I have given the name of *chordal alternation* to a harmonic mannerism quite common in Shepherd's music. It refers not to common practice alternations (as, for example, between tonic and dominant chords) but to special and unusual associations. There is also in Shepherd's alternations a motivic element, similar in a way to motive and phrase-fragment repetitions in Debussy's music.[13] Shepherd usually alternated the chords only two or three times, but as many as six or seven alternations—rarely more—can be found at some places in his music. Often the tonic chord, defining the key, is a member of these progressions, but the chords do not seem to require traditional resolutions. Instead, the harmonic tensions are absorbed in the process of alternation itself. The partwriting is often so smooth as to string the alternating chords together on common tones. These chords may alternate in even or in dotted or otherwise unequal rhythms, but normally the corresponding members of the pair are of equal duration.[14]

Particularly interesting aspects of Shepherd's tonality appear in his modulations. He felt that unusual yet completely convincing modulation was one of the best means open to him for achieving freshness and interest. Many examples, only of passing interest here, are close in conception to the common practice.[15] As one would expect, modulations often occur at the division points within forms; but only rarely does the true modulation by form appear—that is, one in which a cadence in one key and the new phrase in another are completely separate.[16] Shepherd instead provides some kind of connecting link that leads one gently or abruptly, but always convincingly, to the new key.[17]

Of greater importance here are the more intricate, unusual, and individual modulations sprinkled though his music. Shepherd was very fond of the startling modulations obtainable through the chromatic alteration of one or more tones.[18] This chromaticism, often involving enharmonic notation, sometimes includes intervals of the augmented sixth (or diminished third) at the point of the modulation, but Shepherd seldom wrote a typical augmented sixth modulation. Rather, he chose to invert the augmented sixth chord, ignore its traditional resolution, or change its character or that of the chord to which it resolves to something other than the customary types. A beautiful example of some of these aberrations may be seen in the ending of *Most Quietly at Times* (1943)* at the words "it came," where the augmented sixth chord is a half-diminished seventh in the final cadence. Some modulations are best explained by calling attention to the melodic movements in the parts, or to the stressing of a particular tone;[19] and occasionally these occur in rapid succession (see the first page of *Most Quietly at Times*).*

Though unconventional in specific detail, Shepherd's modulations are traditional in that they involve the identification of the tonic or dominant functions of the new key. He often worked with foreign keys, and his attention seems to have been attracted by remote areas of common ground between the keys.

The devices of modal music, chromaticism, and modulation that I have been discussing, and others yet to be discussed, are all related by their common roots in Shepherd's tonality. Except for a handful of passages all his music is essentially tonal, and even these exceptions are set in a milieu of tonality—that is, they consist of contrasting sections, or they are dedicated to the search for their tonality, a search consummated upon arrival at the key. These exceptions first appear in works from the period around 1930. Elsewhere[20] I have presumed to suggest that, having reached fifty years of age, Shepherd may have taken stock of his art and consciously worked at a more up-to-date utterance. In any case he faced the issues straight on. To Percy Goetschius he once wrote that he could not renounce "the necessary *inevitable beauty* of the simpler euphonies."[21] Experiment as he may, he clearly recognized his musical nature for what it was, and he never attempted to speak in what was for him a strange tongue merely to stay abreast of others. In a sketchbook we find this aphorism:

> *Away with esoteric ears! Leave them to donkeys!* If the "innocence of the eye" is a characteristic attribute of the great painter, "innocence" of the ear may account for the most precious moments in music.[22]

The exceptions, those spots that are tonally ambiguous, are tough analytical problems. A passage in *Second Sonata* ("Toccata," meas. 50–61) contains measures that, if controlled in a general way by a five- or six-flat tonality, nevertheless so disregard normal tendencies and so avoid root-designating perfect fifths in the harmonies that the key stands momentarily aside. The *Exotic Dance* (1928; Oxford, 1930), meas. 7–9, hurls foreign harmonies against the melody with such abandon that only the constant oscillation of the tune back to B rescues the key. The separation of the melody and harmony borders on polytonality, as can be seen also in meas. 5 of *Eclogue No. 1*.* The *Prelude* (G minor, 1932)* is an exercise in the integration of nonharmonic tones from a foreign scale, F-sharp minor, into the key such that the whole texture, though aurally understood as dissonant tertian harmony, suggests bitonality to the eye. Aside from short examples of this nature polytonality is not characteristic of Shepherd's style. The only other evidence one finds for it is an occasional polychord, but even there the aural effect is more often a tall tertian, single-rooted dissonance than the dualism implied by the notation.[23]

The limits of Shepherd's nonfunctional writing are found in the *Fantasia on "The Garden Hymn"* (1939) for organ (pp. 8–9), *Quartet for Strings in E Minor* (1933–34) (especially meas. 1–10), and *Lento Amabile* (1938), the latter being the most advanced example of chromaticism in Shepherd's music. There is virtually no modality in the first two and a half pages of this piece. Though some hear C major at the start, there is no underlying diatonic scale. The opening period (meas. 1–8) can also be analyzed in E-flat by reason of its melodic cadence and the overall tonality of the composition. The melody resembles a twelve-tone theme in its avoidance of intervals indicative of tonality, in unpredictable skips and changes of direction, and in the fact that, in a phrase of fifteen tones, all twelve degrees appear. The accompaniment, rising in chromatic major thirds, likewise obscures customary tonal functions. A hint of bitonality occurs in meas. 25–32, where Es and As hold forth, ostinato-like, against encroaching chromatic sequences in the outer voices. The retransition in meas. 35, which returns as a coda, is tonal and is based on a melody clearly perceived in E-flat minor. These two subordinate and essentially diatonic sections within a piece that is prevailingly chromatic in its melodic and harmonic conception reverse the proportions of normal and experimental features noted in his earlier adventures, *Eclogue No. 1** and *Exotic Dance* (Oxford). Their presence reveals, however, that Shepherd never traveled the full distance into chromaticism. The diatonic style was so ingrained that he always kept at least a tenuous hold upon it.

These more adventurous works of the 1930s, in which we find various facets of his experimental urge, are mostly small, and all are composed for instruments. As a group they exhibit the following techniques and characteristics: (1) a greater-than-ordinary freedom of the nonharmonic tones, an adventurousness that impinges upon bitonal preserves; (2) a relatively high percentage of intervallic,

nontertian, and contrapuntal sonorities; (3) nonfunctional root movement; (4) ambiguous tonality, produced by mixtures of keys or by negation of the scale degrees and harmonic devices that define a key; and (5) the creation and support of tonality through contrapuntal and melodic forces rather than harmonic root movement. When the tonal implications of the harmony were too weak Shepherd relied on the melody alone to identify the tonic, dominant, and other significant tonal degrees.

Tough analytical problems, indeed. Does the chromaticism arise from altered nonharmonic tones, modal indicators, or equal partners in a twelve-toned chromatic tonality? It is characteristic of Shepherd's mature style that all three are thoroughly mixed, and it is probably best to consider them as interlocking aspects of a harmonic system that seeks to include the twelve tones and a wide variety of consonant and dissonant sonorities more or less equally within the key. This style is the ultimate expression of the "well-developed sense of tonality" to which Shepherd attributed his harmonic technique. By keeping to the notion of a basic tonality (as I am certain Shepherd did), remembering that he progressively freed himself from reliance on scales and root movement only to create his key, and allowing for stretches in which the key, if not abolished, is temporarily abrogated, one will find that he can understand what is happening, if not explain it. Just as art itself transcends discourse, these passages of music are tonal in ways not yet expressible in words.

A few harmonic devices remain to be discussed. Shepherd's employment of whole-tone chords most often takes the form of a brief intrusion into or interruption of a passage of root movement harmony. Usually a whole-tone chord follows, progresses to, or sometimes even seems to represent a tonic triad. Sometimes it operates to vary the harmonization of a short repeated passage. In vocal works Shepherd found it apt for reference to mysterious aspects of water, wind, moonlight, and so on.[24]

Although pentatonic melodies are not frequent in Shepherd's music, several themes of the four big works that he composed in the 1920s—the Violin Sonata, *Triptych, Horizons,* and *Second Sonata*—do possess pentatonic flavor. Such a theme may also be seen at the beginning of the Piano Quintet (1940). Sometimes Shepherd merely added to a major triad the second and sixth above the root, as on pages 5 and 6 of the full score of *Triptych.* Elsewhere he omitted the third, concentrating on the perfect fourths and fifths, major seconds, and minor sevenths so characteristic of some pentatonic conceptions. These sounds often form good examples of quartal harmony (chords built of fourths) of a pan-diatonic cast. Though nontertian in structure, they nevertheless possess unmistakable aural roots. They can be heard at the opening of the second movement of the Violin Sonata, where Shepherd wrote them in a sparse, rhythmically active texture of seconds and perfect intervals.[25]

Pentatonic and quartal chords usually occur singly. They so frequently imply familiar progressions that Shepherd may have produced them merely by altering more familiar harmonies. *Horizons* opens with a chord—spelled upwards G, A, C, D—that for this piece fulfills the tonic function even more colorfully than would the tonic triad itself. Quartal harmonies appear on the first page of *Processionale Festivo** in about as high a concentration as one should expect in Shepherd's music; there they participate in tonality-forming root movements. The last five measures of *Eclogue* (1948; Presser 1956) fashion a plagal cadence from nontertian sounds. Occasionally Shepherd emphasized quartal harmonies by repeating or lengthening them to two, three, or more measures. Much of this is reminiscent of certain music of Paul Hindemith, whose style and theoretical writings loomed before Shepherd as examples of responsible modernity.[26]

In a few compositions Shepherd used major or minor seconds to accentuate a rhythmic pattern or to blur a melodic outline; however, he did not write tone clusters such as those of Henry Cowell and Charles Ives. The most forceful examples of accent by the use of seconds will be found in the "Toccata" of *Second Sonata* and in *Two Step.** A rare case of major seconds used for their atmospheric, impressionistic quality occurs in meas. 56–58 of the song *Reverie,** where they evoke the stillness of the scene described in the text.

The repeating or lengthening of a chord is a definite point of style that Shepherd must have enjoyed. His effect is the cessation of harmonic rhythm, a hiatus in which one or more melodies are set to repeating or developing themselves. In addition to the quartal harmonies mentioned above, various other dissonant or unstable chords appear. In these situations the tonality resides in the root of the sustained chord or in the tonal implications of the melodic parts.[27] Sometimes, as at the beginning of *Nocturne,** the tonality-anchoring function is entrusted not to physically long durations but to repeatedly stressed or accented tones.[28] A fascinating combination of these effects occurs at the beginning of *The Starling Lake* (1944), where a repeated minor third (A-C) tethers the tonality against the ever-shifting tonal allegiance of an artificial scale of alternating half- and whole steps. The intervallic nature of this scale, which occurs in several works, allies it closely with the diminished seventh chord, but Shepherd's harmonizations invariably hide it.[29]

A still more subtle device for the overall control and regulation of harmonic events through large sections of a form can be called the *structural tone*, a term which I use to describe the continuous influence of a particular degree through a lengthy passage. The A-flat at the beginning of the slow movement of the Violin Sonata is an example. Structural tones may be continuously present or intermittent. They may remain in place or appear in different octave registers. They may be melody tones, chord tones, nonharmonic tones, pedal tones, or long continuous roots. Ostinato passages stressing a structural tone frequently account in part for the harmonic shape of a phrase. The more intriguing of them appear in various and constantly changing harmonic or textural guises. Their mere presence rather than their harmonic or melodic roles seems to account for their influence.

Though I am not certain that he was aware of them, structural tones occur in many works from all periods of Shepherd's writing. One of the most sensitive and subtle will be found in the song *Virgil*. The tone is D-flat (C-sharp), commencing in meas. 22 and lasting until meas. 62. It begins as the dominant of G-flat major. Throughout the passage D-flat controls the melodic boundaries, climaxes, and cadences of the vocal melody. It is constantly present as a harmonic factor, whether the progressions are functional or nonfunctional. There is no doubt in my mind that the amazing effect of the tritone cadence in the setting of the word "tomb" derives not only from its relation to the text, but also from the obliteration of a structural tone that has been at work for forty measures. A not-dissimilar cadence will be found at the end of *Most Quietly at Times.**

Shepherd seldom spoke or wrote about music at any length without touching on the subject of rhythm. It was particularly evident in his approach to vocal composition, a topic on which he expressed himself very clearly and which I discussed fully in Chapter 5. His views on the rhythmic nature of instrumental writing normally appeared in a discussion of harmony, counterpoint, texture, or form; and so far as I am aware he never formulated them into a definite and organized statement. But in the absence of dogma his sensitivity and the spirit of his approach to rhythm are adequate substitutes.

> Then the *Quintet*.[30] This I feel is one of my best works. Look in particular at the rhythmic structure at the beginning of the slow movement and recall Tovey's dictum "Ambiguity is an aesthetic fact." I'd like to make a whole lecture on that declaration; so seemingly paradoxical in its implication but also so pregnant with suggestiveness in music. . . .
>
> In all my vocal compositions, the matter of prosody and all rhythmical features should claim first attention. I think and hope that your own understanding of *metre* per se and *rhythm* and their interplay is sufficient to put you on *my* trail. It would require nothing short of a dissertation, well illustrated, to convey my ideas in this field. There are so many ramifications! Our 19th century outlook (in this regard) was frightfully astigmatic! And on the theoretical and didactic fronts, our mentors went far astray. . . .
>
> It may be that the chief musical assets of the present era are in the domain of rhythm, or shall I say in an alerted awareness of rhythmical forms, syntax, nuances. This awareness is also greatly in evidence in contemporary poetry. . . .
>
> An entirely different "Kettle of fish" is the Invitation to the Dance. Now I happen to know that this is *just* dandy! (Ask Jimmy Aliferis[31] about it.) Once more: take a good gander at the *rhythm* of the opening line "Spread the board etc." then keep your nose close to the prosody throughout! Anyhow that's how I got my fun out of it.[32]

One further interesting bypath deserves consideration: Shepherd's relationship to twelve-tone music. Though one would not expect him to embrace Schoenberg's method—he was much too tonal for that—he did, nevertheless, know the system. In his teaching notes one encounters short exercises in twelve-tone style, and the theme of *Lento Amabile*, his least tonal work, uses all twelve degrees. Still, the closest analogy is evident in the opening theme of the third movement of *Quartet for Strings No. 4* (1955). This twelve-note theme is announced by the second violin, answered in the viola, and restated from time to time during the movement. Could Shepherd have been toying with the method? I think not. Overall there is no serial manipulation of the notes. It is possible that this lovely melody came into being through a span of conscious rumination on the twelve-tone method, but beyond that we cannot detect it; for the theme was absorbed into habitual patterns of thought.

By now we see that Arthur Shepherd employed a wide range of harmonic techniques. He broadened the customary tertian-tonal harmony by the inclusion of modal, whole-tone, and chromatic procedures. He was interested in nontertian sonorities and in pentatonic themes and figurations. He penned relatively long sections, the harmonic activity of which is controlled by structural tones. Excepting chromaticism, the modal and nontertian are the most frequent of these devices, but all exist only in limited usage. I have not been able to discover any system or order in which these devices occur. Why did Shepherd use a brief whole-tone passage on page 3 of *Processionale Festivo*?* One may satisfy himself that it was to break up the influence of structural tone, G, that pervades the preceding measures, or that it was meant to serve as a foil to the nontertian sonorities that precede it. In my opinion, Shepherd was not systematic in the use of these rarer harmonic methods; they seem simply to have occurred to him from time to time for relief, for variety, or for still other reasons. He possessed a remarkable ability to integrate them into a work so expertly that they never distract, but belong.

COUNTERPOINT

In my studies of Shepherd's music three aspects of counterpoint have attracted my particular attention. One of these, the lightly contrapuntal employment of motives, imitation, and ostinato, enlivens and lightens his textures. Its obvious influence so permeates almost all the music in these volumes that it seems necessary merely to draw it to the reader's attention. Another, his use of the formal contrapuntal devices and forms, will be discussed later. At present, then, I want to draw attention to the harmonic nature of Shepherd's counterpoint, its role in his partwriting, and its influence on his sonorities (chords) and progressions.

In Chapter 7 I pointed out the totally traditional counterpoint to be found in the *Fugue in C-sharp Minor.** Though Shepherd seldom adhered so closely to the style of Bach's music, there are other works whose technique differs only in slight degree from the common practice.[33] Still, in *The Fiddlers* (1932), to some extent in *Reverie,** but prominently in *Gigue Fantasque* (1931) Shepherd made use of a diatonic, scale-oriented tonality that may be considered the contrapuntal manifestation of his modal style. It is not unlike Stravinsky's pan-diatonic passages, though harmonically it is more functional and is usually limited to a two-part texture. The general characteristics of this music are: (1) an increase in free dissonances, though the common nonharmonic tones still are present; (2) a higher percentage, or at least more obvious use, of perfect intervals on accents; (3) the occasional employment of a quite ambiguous implied harmony, including nontertian sonorities; (4) a tonality resulting largely from melodic motivation along the prevailing scale (quite often, when the harmony is noncommital, a melodic stress of the first, third, or fifth tones of the scale is employed to create the tonic); and (5) freer partwriting—a casual attitude toward the resolution of

dissonances as well as the use of consecutive perfect fourths, fifths, and octaves.

There are also contrapuntal examples of the more experimental or abstruse harmony.[34] In the beginning of *Exotic Dance No. 3* (1941; rev. 1956),* for example, all the modes are combined into a scale of twelve tones in which only the tonic and dominant serve as the guardians of the key. Still, after the first cadence in score 3, the chords are more definitely implied, the root movements become unambiguous, and a more traditional fit between melody and accompanying harmony is in evidence.[35]

The care that Shepherd lavished upon his partwriting is evident; with regard to it William S. Newman observed: "I would say that skilful partwriting is one of the chief signs of his outstanding—really outstanding—craftsmanship."[36] In a similar vein Shepherd took special interest in contrapuntal manipulation of materials. His piano music, for example, reveals his fondness for snatches of imitation, obbligato melodies, and motive development. Like Chopin he did not bind himself to consistency in the number of voices he employed, the integrity or faithfulness of his imitations, or other niceties of academic polyphony. Nor did he explore systematically the traditional methods of contrapuntal elaboration and development; instead, he was inclined to employ certain of them and to virtually ignore others. One observes a liberal use of contrary motion in the development of motives and themes, considerable reliance on ostinato as a constructional device, and widespread employment of simple imitation; by contrast, diminution and augmentation, retrograde motion, invertible counterpoint, and the application of contrary motion to these devices are rare, each existing in only one or two examples. Furthermore, their use is more often free than strict, the contrapuntal effect depending on a similarity of shapes rather than on the correspondence of details.

The third movement of *Horizons* must be cited in connection with these remarks. In it Shepherd depicted the activity, the fun and humor, the work and bustle of range life, settlement life, and rural and mountain life. The two cowboy songs on which the movement is based—"The Old Chisholm Trail" and "As I was a-walking one morning for pleasure"—are worked into a large *a b a* form, whose structure is defined by the sections devoted to the two melodies. The tunes are handled on variation principles, simply stated in a few instruments and gradually worked up to some grand climaxes. Canonic variations are employed in the first part, while in the second, contrary motion and mirror devices are prominent. In the third section, a recapitulation, decorations and embellishments both of theme and texture are utilized.

In the opening section Shepherd worked merely in canonic imitations of isolated phrases of the tune, canons that in their light, scherzaic quality add much to the humor of the movement. In the second movement of *Second Sonata*, a theme with variations, there are a number of more intricate and extended examples of canonic imitation. The first variation, *Con severità e chiarezza*, is a rigorous exercise that sets each phrase in triple or quadruple canon, utilizing various intervals and distances as well as a few imitations by contrary motion. A characteristic repeated-note motive that pervades this variation aids the ear in identifying the canons. Whereas a similar phrase form of canon imitation also occurs in *Fantasia on "The Garden Hymn,"* its third variation (*Tempo del tema; tranquillamente*) is marked by a consistency of canonic writing that approaches the normal state of the device, that of continuous strict imitation throughout a section or work. Here, curiously, the canonic melody is the retrograde form of "The Garden Hymn."

Though Shepherd rarely employed invertible counterpoint, an example may be found in the fifth of "The Garden Hymn" variations (*Leggiero*). The form is ternary (*a, b a, b^1 a*) with written-out repeats. Parts *b* and b^1 are inverted sections;[37] a delicate and pleasing relationship. The most ingenious example of intricate counterpoint that I have discovered in Shepherd's music exists in a pair of passages from *Gigue Fantasque* in which an inversion of intervals is produced by contrary motion without register inversion of the two parts.[38] Owing to his typical disregard for integrity of detail (in this respect his counterpoint resembles that of Handel rather than Bach) the relationship is actually an illusion. The device is evoked by a general correspondence in the shapes of the two passages. Shepherd's intent is clear, his means free, the result well wrought.

TEXTURE

Second Sonata occupies a central position in Shepherd's music for the piano, revealing textures common to early as well as late works. Earlier works—the *Sonata*, Op. 4; *Sonata for Pianoforte and Violin;* the accompaniments to the songs *The Gentle Lady,* Oh, Like a Queen's Her Happy Tread** (1922), and *Where Loveliness Keeps House**—are all written with sonorous tertian chords enlivened by clever keyboard figurations. In his later music the pianism is more varied as he adapted many other textures to serve his expressive needs. Pianists have remarked on the "athleticism" or "athletic challenge" of this music. Shepherd played with a loose, leggiero keyboard technique and pedaled richly. His fingerings frequently take the hand away from notated sustained tones, which must then be held by the pedal.

The first page of *Scherzino** reveals a typical fondness for "filler tones" between the notes of a melody. A desire for rhythmic vitality, sparkling sonority, and contrapuntal interest influences most of his writing for the piano, *allegro* or *adagio.* As an accompaniment to lyrical melodies Shepherd sometimes used quasi-ostinato patterns, particularly good examples of which occur in the song *Reverie,** and the first and third *Eclogues** for piano. Occasionally he doubled a melody at the octave or fifteenth, with harmonic notes distributed lightly about and between the parallel lines.[39] In some works one encounters an almost traditional technique of motive development,[40] in others a rather strict web of two- or three-part counterpoint. *Gigue Fantasque* is Baroque in texture though not in harmony. To illustrate a more contemporary idiom I would cite the "Toccata" from *Second Sonata, Two Step,* Capriccio No. 2* (1941) and *Exotic Dance No. 3,** in which the writing is often dry, sparse, even percussive. A purely chordal texture is very rare. A peculiarity of Shepherd's notation is his use of the harmonic sign of string notation, which he mentioned having seen also in the piano music of Manuel Infante. The interpretation of these harmonics can usually be inferred from the context; in *The Gentle Lady** they refer to "laughing bells."[41] They are always played on the keys—he never reached inside the piano in an attempt to produce a true harmonic on the string—thus the notation suggests an effect rather than a method of creating the tone.

Whereas the texture of *Triptych* tends toward the homophonic style, the other works for string quartet—including the Piano Quintet—achieve a greater degree of equality among the four instruments. This was accomplished by placing individual instruments in relief against the others and by liberal use of contrapuntal or motive-development textures. The choral works use customary methods on the whole, with the *Invitation to the Dance* somewhat more individual and adventurous than the others. Here we find part doublings in octaves, and the use of selected voices alone or in pairs. Nothing is unusual, but all is so competent and effective that one readily recognizes the hand of a master. The choral scores are full of intricate and delicate detail, either among the parts themselves or with the accompaniment or text. The ending of the *Invitation,* beginning perhaps at the double bar on page 9, is a particularly good example.

Shepherd's orchestral writing bespeaks the familiarity with orchestral literature he gained from his experience as a conductor. His employment of the instruments is in line with nineteenth-century practice—very competent but with little tendency toward individuality. I think his conservatism arose partly from the essentially abstract character of his music. It is true that in the sketches of *Horizons* one can find penciled remarks such as "Woodwinds: howling of the wind and bleakness of the prairee." These suggest Impressionistic thinking, yet in the score as it now stands the instruments seem to react more strongly to musical logic than to the descriptive or pictorial representations that so often in the history of music have engendered new effects. Furthermore Shepherd, a pianist, did not himself play any orchestral instrument, and he tended to be cautious in his demands upon players. He normally wrote for the standard symphony orchestra, occasionally with extra instruments. In *Horizons,* for example, he added a tenor saxophone for the solos in the second movement, "The Lone Prairee," as well as a fourth bassoon, trumpets to a total of five, piano, and organ.[42]

The strings were the backbone of Shepherd's orchestra. He employed woodwinds for touches of color and occasional solos (especially the oboe), for melodic doubling of other instruments, for rapid octave and unison passage work, for the brilliance of quick and high figuration, and to add body to the tutti. The brasses seldom speak individually or as an independent section. Single brass instruments occasionally associate with strings or woodwinds, but in the main they add power and richness to the ensemble or murmur soft chords in harmonic support of other instruments. The percussion is almost entirely devoted to rhythmic support and the delineation of rhythmic patterns; there are few percussion solos.

FORM

What are the fundamental conditions essential to most of Shepherd's music? It is tuneful—purposely so—both as to original melodies and occasional borrowed themes. He used this obvious thematicism to clarify his forms. It is tonal. It adheres to the dramatic, developmental, symphonic idea of form that is the heritage of Beethoven as modified by Shepherd's great love for Bach, by his natural affinity for the music of the early twentieth-century French composers, and by the lessons he learned from writing songs.

The patterns he used are many and varied. The piano pieces in this book are mostly cast along lines defined by the Romantic composers and described by Percy Goetschius, with whose form-texts Shepherd was so familiar. On the other hand they do not adhere exactly to any of the ingredients or proportions Goetschius prescribed. Shepherd's smaller ternaries often vary the return of opening materials in ways that assure a continually rising curve of intensity. He particularly enjoyed altering traditional features of ternary form. In "He It Is" from *Triptych* a ternary pattern is formed from two similar, short sections separated by through-composed sections rather than "versified," contrasting materials. "The Lone Prairee" (second movement of *Horizons*) places its theme, "The Dying Cowboy," as a tenor saxophone solo at the beginning and end. The effect is ternary, but merely to label it such would be misleading, for these outer sections are too small to bear the weight normally given to *a* sections. Nor are they separated by contrasting thematic material, but by contrasting treatment of the theme itself in the form of thematic development: a fantasia in eight sections. Another altered ternary form—*a b c* a^1—appears in the second movement of the Piano Quintet. Here *b* and *c*, despite the contrast implied by their letter designations, are permeated by allusions to *a*; and a^1 likewise refers to events of the preceding sections.

In my discussion of Shepherd's use of canonic imitation and inversion I have already had opportunity to speak of his variations, for his employment of such devices occurred more naturally in the context of variations than in forms customarily perused in search of ingenious counterpoint. (He seems to have been disinterested in fugues, chorale preludes, passacaglias, and the like as independent forms.) There are at least two and probably three works that employ the traditional form of theme and variations: *Theme and Variations* (c. 1903, for piano), which I have been unable to study, the second movement of *Second Sonata*, and *Variations on an Original Theme* for orchestra (1951–52). In the latter two the relationship of the variations to their theme is never obscured, since it was Shepherd's opinion that "the variations should be on easy speaking terms with the theme."[43] The writing in these works fairly well sums up his use of variation technique everywhere: (1) contrapuntal elaboration of the material in canon or invertible counterpoint, as described above; (2) decorative melodic embellishment of the theme; and (3) the use of contrary motion and motive variation to produce new thematic material. Three other works, *Fantasia on "The Garden Hymn,"* *Quintet for Pianoforte and Strings* (second movement), and *Sonata for Pianoforte and Violin* also employ these techniques, as distinct from formal variations, in the treatment of themes within a movement.

The *Variations on an Original Theme*, Shepherd's last work for orchestra, is also his final essay in large-scale variation form. He desired to write orchestral music possessed of the seriousness of purpose and the elements of contrast, development, dénouement, and conclusion one expects in a symphonic work. Thus he shaped the successive variations to serve architecturally and dramatically as the various themes, transitions, and other parts of a symphonic movement. Of necessity he avoided the light salon variations (in his words, "grab-bag variations") that the term "theme and variations" can so easily connote; yet, desiring coherence, he also shunned the highly transmuted types which claim their relationships to the theme only through intermediary elements. The form is not new. There is little in the work that could be called new, yet it is full of interesting and expressive features. It proposes a subject on which it discusses gracefully according to familiar principles, exploring its implications with ingenuity and interest. It instructs and entertains through sober employment of an old and honored art. By contrast, the variations in *Second Sonata*, though not light, are of the more traditional cut of successive arrangements each in essentially the same form as the theme.

In *Second Sonata*, written about 1930, we note the appearance of a disciplined and tidy mode of thought particularly evident in the economy of materials in the form. The first movement is especially compact and ideally proportioned. Of all Shepherd's large works it is one of the closest to traditional patterns. The relative popularity of *Second Sonata* results from its fine craftsmanship as well as the beauty of its style and thematic material. It is an effective work, not so emotional as the Violin Sonata yet appealing and gratifying to play.

The first and last movements of *Second Sonata* are written in sonata form, the influence of which is great in Shepherd's instrumental music. Though a number of more or less traditional sonata forms may be cited,[44] clear-cut unequivocal examples are not the rule. For example, many movements in his sonatas, as well as his single-movement works, mix sonata form with other patterns.[45] Just as his attention in analysis was usually given to unique aspects of a form, so did he alter traditional patterns in his own music; and the variety of forms that has resulted is among the most fascinating aspects of his music.

In general, his sonata forms have no introduction. The first subjects are long melodic arches: extended phrases or periods with few interior cadences. Often they are wholly or partially repeated, either immediately or after a bit of intervening material. Transitions may be similar to or grow out of the first subject, or they may be quite independent and individual. Second subjects are usually sectional, containing two or more ideas; and this material is often well contrasted with the foregoing music. In *Overture to a Drama,* for example, the emotional second subject group (p. 14 at rehearsal number 5) provides lyric contrast to a robust first subject. "Toccata" (*Second Sonata*), on the other hand, marks the second subject by changes in texture, melodic patterns, and harmonic character, without altering the tempo or rhythmic character of the movement.

His development sections have few characteristics in common beyond a tendency toward sectional construction. Sometimes Shepherd fashioned an entire development out of just one subject. Frequently he drew more widely from among the materials of the exposition. In some cases the development seems only tenuously related to the exposition. Perhaps this means new themes have appeared. (One cannot always believe that the ingenuity of the analyst in relating and deriving materials correctly reflects the evolutionary process the composer followed in creating them.) The recapitulations tend to compress material by shortening or omitting themes and transitions, but thematic events normally recur in the original order, and the time-honored principle of a change of tonality in the second subject area is observed—though not to the point of using the customary key relationships. Quite often the structure of a subject is altered, particularly if it was originally composed of two or more ideas. In extreme cases Shepherd rewrote a wholly new and equivalent, but not parallel, recapitulation out of the materials of the exposition.

Interesting deviations from the obvious may be found in the recapitulations of *Second Sonata.* That of the first movement (p. 6, score 4) makes a curious return to the middle rather than the beginning of the first phrase, producing a glimmer of recognition that ripens into positive identification with the arrival of the second phrase. The first subject of "Toccata" (the last movement), consisting of several consecutive developments of a phrase-idea, returns in the recapitulation in the guise of yet further developments, a technique also used in "The Old Chisholm Trail" from *Horizons,* the second movement of the Violin Sonata, and the Piano Quintet.

Imaginative arrangement and variation of his materials are more original elements of Shepherd's music than the melodic and harmonic aspects of the materials themselves. For this reason his music seems more admirable after study than upon one hearing only. Apparently his forms grew as the materials were hammered into shape. His desire to communicate with his audience led him to search for arrangements and relationships of musical ideas that would satisfy on both emotional and intellectual planes. He did not consciously attempt to create new forms but moved freely within the forms handed down to him, secure in his knowledge of the license exercised by the masters and the workings of his own talent and imagination. His works frequently mix the characteristics of one form with another, and some seem to be truly unique structures. In surveying all of Shepherd's music one leans toward the notion that it was formed less from patterns bequeathed to him than under the influence of principles which interact in varying proportion from work to work—principles of tonality, unity, cyclic form, contrast, development, and variation. Through this approach I can best account for the great variety of forms and formal details that one encounters, and I want to discuss these points briefly by way of review and summary.

Except for a section here or there the force of tonality is strong in Shepherd's music. It is one of his links with the past. He used it for contrast and confirmation, for relief and return. The majority of his compositions end in the same center ("key" does not always seem applicable) in which they begin, and the recapitulation of the opening material is likewise "in the tonic." The few exceptions to these precepts lead to one's awareness of how often they are followed. Apparently there are no restrictions on the choice of keys that constitute the tonal pattern of a composition. Wide and frequent—sometimes rampant—modulation characterizes some of the music. Even in short works one finds modulations to far-distant centers (whether measured by the interval between their key tones or the relationship of their signatures). On the other hand there is a healthy use of the nearly related keys of the Baroque and Classic periods, and Shepherd was sometimes content with sections that remain consistently within one or two keys—a trait that provided Denoe Leedy with critical ammunition.[46]

Shepherd's music is unified in conventional ways. Tonality partly explains the cohesion of these works, but perhaps the most obvious unifying element is the thematic material on which his music is based. He himself often remarked on his predilection for tunes and for customary methods of thematic treatment. On the other hand, his mature instrumental melodies are seldom the kind that one remembers and whistles after only one hearing. The jagged outlines, dissonant intervals, and speedy rhythms deliver the music from an excess of lyricism.

Cyclic form—the use of thematic material in more than one movement of a composition—is typical of Shepherd's sonatas, quartets, and symphonies. Usually the first subject of the first movement recurs in later movements as a contrasting theme, as transitional material, or as the finale. The third movement of *Second Sonata,* for example, is based on the subject of the first; and the "Toccata," to which the third movement stands as a short introduction, is based on yet another rhythmic variation of the same motive. The initial motive of the *Sonata for Pianoforte and Violin* also recurs in later movements. Moreover, its first four pitches announce the key tones of the respective movements. This is only one, though the most extensive, of the cyclic patterns in this work. Others in which cyclical themes occur are *Horizons, Quartet for Strings in E Minor, Quintet for Pianoforte and Strings,* and the *Quartet for Strings No. 4.*

Contrast is achieved both by the use of new themes and by a new treatment of old themes. In the larger works Shepherd provides considerable contrast between sections, but the smaller instrumental works and most of the songs relate their successive sections to each other in generally similar tempos and rhythms. Paradoxically, Shepherd sometimes achieves greater contrast when a new section is a variation of a preceding one than when it makes use of new material.

Development is very common not only in development sections as such but also in areas where thematic material is presented, restated, or recapitulated. Shepherd considered economy of thematic material a habit of the old masters worthy of emulation, and he took an almost sinful pride in his ability to develop long passages out of his materials. His marked talent for spinning out small ideas may be seen, for example, in the phrase extensions of *Gigue Fantasque.* Recapitulations are likely to be so richly developed that they amount virtually to a new working-out of the original material. Variation of themes occurs not only in formal sets of variations but as a method of thematic development. Shepherd often extended sections by the use of successively different textures and melodic variations of a phrase. I have noted several works in which a theme, when repeated or recapitulated, reappears as a tiny group of variations that fulfills a function in the form normally entrusted to a single statement of the theme.

Motivic development and variations of themes interact so closely that one cannot always distinguish between them in analysis. Together they may produce such severe changes in the character of the thematic material that one may regard it as having assumed an essentially new form, as though through metamorphosis. Gradual mutation of the material in this manner occasionally appears in Shepherd's through-composed songs; an example is *Virgil.* Its melodic and accompaniment motives go through a continual process of growth into new objects, all of the same ethos, such that the last is a logical and necessary result of the first, although the relationship between them might go unrecognized were the intervening steps removed.

With these few general statements of analysis, this necessarily brief discussion of Arthur Shepherd and his music comes to its end. Its brevity is intentional, in order to devote sufficient space to something yet more important: the music that spawned it. Shepherd's story needs to be told, and some interpretive remarks seem appropriate; but in his chosen field Shepherd was supremely able to speak for himself.

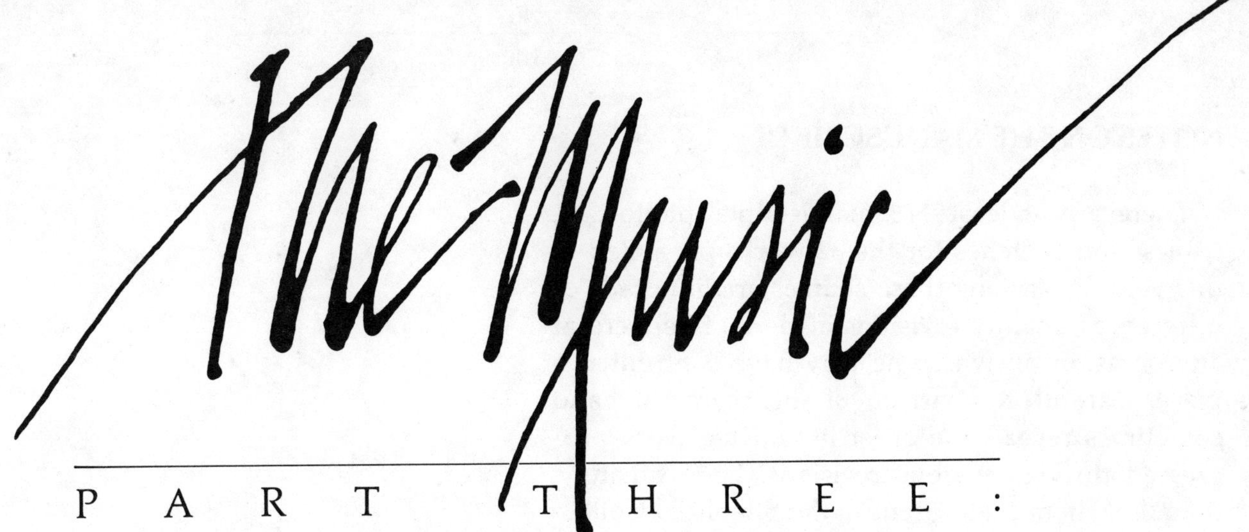

PART THREE:

NOTES ON THE MANUSCRIPTS

There are at least 115 manuscripts, photostats, copies, and sketches for the 32 works presented in this volume. Among these sources are hundreds of differences, mainly revisions made by Shepherd at any occasion on which he may have confronted a piece. Careful comparison of the scores at hand sometimes reveals the order in which a work progressed through various revisions. Unfortunately, not all of them are present in the Shepherd Collection. Gaps in the history of a work appear, and many seem to be unbridgeable. Thus certain works exist in two or more equally definitive, or unreliable, versions, depending on how one looks at them. Faced with this situation, I have simply done the best I could. I think that we have copied the best manuscripts available. Notes on a few special cases follow.

Fugue for the Pianoforte in C-sharp Minor. A revision, found in the score, is given on page 75. It fits into page 5, as shown by the crossed circles, and it probably substitutes for the next three measures.

Fugue, C-sharp Minor

2.
subito pp ed espress
cresc.
p
p
cresc
f
a tempo, ma tranquillo
3

3.
Ped
mf marc.
f
Ped
sempre f
sempre marcato

poco accel.
sempre f
re-strike at intervals
f

rit.
pp
Cresc poco a poco
Sempre cresc
allarg.
Maestoso
ff
cresc
8va

6.
sempre ff al fine.
6/20/22
Cleveland O.

(P.S. score 2 → Score A)
found in score A
[A.S. Fugue in c# minor] Item C
8va bassa
8va

Prelude in B-flat Minor, page 3, score 3, measure 1, fourth beat: I believe that Shepherd meant A-natural.

Score A
Prelude
Allegro
R.H
L.H
Ped
Ped.
8va
sub pp

2.
poco rubato
pp
f
mf
p
Ped
R.H
L.H

3.
f
ff
pp
pp
p
p
L.H.

4.
sempre legato
poco rit
May 9, 1931

Score C
correct version
Eclogue No 1.
Arthur Shepherd
Allegretto piacevole ♩. = 84
mf
Ped.
poco trattenuto
pp
poco accel.
a tempo primo
mf
poco rit.
a tempo
p

gliss.
8va
pp
mp
R. H
L. H.
mf
accel
a tempo
pp
p
cresc.
mf
f

L.
R.
f
mf
p
f
R.H.
f
p
mf
p
mf
pp
pp
poco slentando
a tempo
p
mf

5

Prelude
A. Shepherd
Lento espressivo ♪=72
pp
legato
mf
f
Ped
Ped
Ped

2.
f
Ped
L.H.
L.H.
Cresc.
f
R.H
L.H
R.H
f
dim
rit.
a tempo
p
L.H.

3
pp
L.H.
mp
mf
p
pp
June 29, 1932.

Capriccio No. 1. The correct order of the numbered pages is 1, 2, 4, 3, 5. Somehow Shepherd must have mixed the pages when he bound them, then numbered them. Three other manuscripts, as well as internal evidence, support this conclusion.

Exotic Dance II (page 97). There are three sources: two early holographs and a poor facsimile of one of them by my copying process (hereafter called RL process). Shepherd revised the latter, so the reproduction of it contained here is not as clear as I had hoped. With it were found the two revisions given on page 96, one of which is the beginning of a new clean copy.

Score D
Capriccio No. I
R. Shepherd.
Allegro mod^to. ma energicamente ♩=96
cresc.
8va
legg.

2 ..

Capr #1

poco meno mosso
Ped.
espress.
poco più mosso
Capr #1

(See catalogue card regarding order of pages - RNL) 3

Capr #1

8va
sub. p
dim
8va bassa
Nov. 7, 1938
(Revised, Aug. 18, 1941)
over for two pianos!
or Orchestra
Capr #1

(Exotic Dance No 2)
Item D
found in Score C

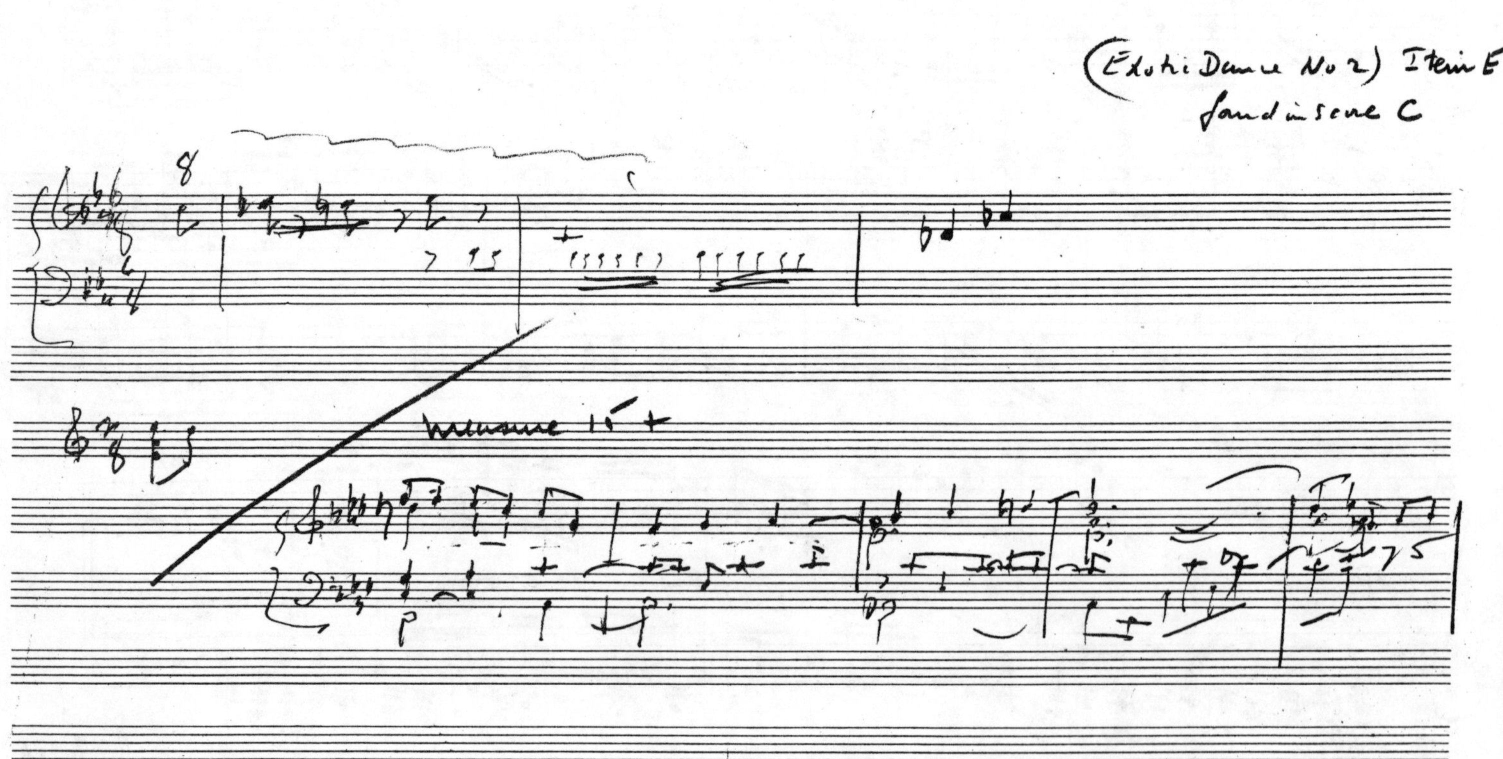
(Exotic Dance No 2) Item E
found in Score C
measure 15 +

Score C

A. S.

1'

2.

Exotic Dance #2

Exotic Dance #2

Exotic Dance #2

Score A
Two Step
A. Shepherd
Allegro Modto.
♩=100

2.

3

4

5

6

1941
Correct
Score C
♩. = 54
♪ = 152
Nocturne
A. Shepherd
Tranquillamente
mf ben cantando
mf
cresc.
f
p
mf
ten.
mp
mf
mp
f
f
poco cresc.
ff
mp
Ped

2

dim e rall.
a tempo
pp
mf
dim.
ten.
poco agitato
mp
pp
mf
sempre più agitato
p
mf
f
f
p
f
p
leggerissimo
f

Nocturne

3

Nocturne

Nocturne

Exotic Dance No. 3
R. Shepherd.
1.
Score D
Allegretto con grazia ♩ = 96
mf
Very legato
mf
mp
mf
mf
mp
mf
mf
mf

2.

Exotic Dance No 3

3

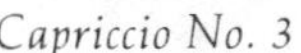

Score A

1

Capriccio No. 3

R. Shepherd

Allegro ♩. = 76

poco allarg.

a tempo

2.

a tempo
poco rit.
f
sf
Capr #3

4.

Score C
2
Scherzino
R. Shepherd.
Vivace e secco ♩. = 69
mf
f
mf
ff
8va
p
f
f
p
mf

2

3

dim.
pp
mf
pp
mf
f
8va
f
f
Rit.
f
pp sotto voce
ppp
cresc.
poco affret.

4

5

Score A
Souvenir
R. S.
Andantino teneramente
Mar. 10, 1945

Score C
Souvenir
R. Sheppard
Andantino teneramente ♩=76
mp
mf
p
poco rall.
a tempo
To
Mar. 10/45

Souvenir (page 124). Two versions have been copied, a comparison of which shows Shepherd in a typical revising mood.

Score C
Processionale Festivo
R. Shephers
alla marcia 𝅗𝅥 = 84

2.

3.

4
legg.
mp
f
8va
ff
f
dim.
poco
a
poco
mp
p
come lontano
8
dim.
pp
f
ff

correct version
Eclogue No. 3
A. S.
Score A
Andantino ♩ = 69
mp
espress.
mf
poco più animato
mf
f

2.

3
poco ra
8va
Oct. 26, 1949

Sun Down. The turtle at the top of the page was Shepherd's identifying mark on the score *The Lost Child* in the National Music Clubs Contest in 1909, and probably indicates that *Sun Down* was also entered in that or another competition.

To Miss. Edna C. Cohn.

Sun Down

Poem by William Ernest Henley

Arthur Shepherd

Score

2

rene, — a shin-ing peace — — —
The smoke as-cends in a rosy and gold-en
haze — — — The spires shine and are chang'd In the
val-ley sha — dows rise —
sf p
sf
mp

3.
The lark sings on
The
sun clos-ing his ben-e-dic-tion sinks
And the
misterioso
crescendo
dark-ning air thrills with a
cresc

sense of the tri-um-phing night.
night with her train of stars and her
allargando
great gift of sleep.
molto rit.
espress
parlando
So be my pas-sing

5

G
p
molto espressivo
my task ac-com-plished and the
pp
Ped.
sempre
long day done. my wa-ges
poco cresc.
Ped.
ta-ken and in my heart some late lark
sing-ing.
Ped.

6

p ben legato
Let me be gathered to the
sempre ped.
qui- - - et West -
the
sun - down splendid and se - rene

mf
rit.
Death.
p
p
dim.
8va
8va
ppp
8va
8va

Sunday up the River
James Thomson
R. Shepherd
Tranquillo ♩=72
mp
The church bells are ringing How green the earth
Come campani
mf
mp
p
how fresh and fair.
The thrush-es are singing What
f
p
mf
rapt — ure but to breathe this air.
The
espress.
mp
church bells are ring-ing
mp Sognando
Lo how the riv - er dream-eth there
pp

The thrushes are singing. Green flames wave lightly
Fervidamente
ev'-ry-where. The church bells are ring-ing, the thrushes are singing, How
all the world breathes praise and prayer. What Sab-bath peace doth trance the
air
1912

WRU
Barnwell

Score A.

"He Came All so Still" c. 1950

Andante semplice

p He came all so still, where his moth-er was

mp As dew in Ap-rill that fall-eth, fall-eth on the grass

p He came all so still, where his mother lay, as dew in

Ap-rill, that fall-eth on the spray

espress.

p He came all so

2.

still, to his moth-er's bower As dew in Ap-rill that fall-eth
espress.
fall-eth on the flower Moth-er and maid-en was
mf
pp
nev-er none but She Well might such a lad-y
f
mf
God's moth-er be, God's moth - er be.
pp
ppp

The Gentle Lady. Between the time that I photographed the song in Cleveland—the score that Shepherd approved—and the summer of 1958 when I catalogued the Shepherd Collection, the definitive score disappeared. The version in my dissertation is correct, but the RL process was too crude to be usable here. This is the next-to-last stage of the work—referring, of course, to revisions made since publication of *The Gentle Lady* in *The Art of Music* in 1916.

To my Sister, Josephine
Score F
The Gentle Lady
John Masefield
Arthur Shepherd
Tempo di minuetto ♩ = 88
So beau-ti-ful, so dain-ty sweet, So like a lyre's de-light-ful touch, A beauty per-fect, ripe com-plete That art's own hand could on-ly smutch, And nat-ure's self not bet-ter much
poco cresc.
espress.
poco rit
pochiss. rit
a tempo
So beau-ti-ful, So pure-ly wrought, Like a

(A. Shepherd, The Gentle Lady) Score F p.2
mf poco rall.
a tempo
mp
fair mis-sal penned with hymns. So gent-le, so sur-pas — sing thought,
A beaut-eous soul, in love-ly limbs, A lant-ern that an ang - el trims.
cresc.
So simp-le sweet, with-out a sin, Like gentle mus-ic gent-ly timed, Like

(A.S., The Gentle Lady) Score F p3.
mf
ten.
Thyme words com-ing apt-ly in, To round a moon-ed poem rhymed, To tunes the laugh-ing bells have
mf
mp
p
chimed.
pp
ppp

1
Score A
"Oh like a queen's her happy tread"
em by
William Watson.
Andante a l'improvvisata ma sonoramente
mf

2.
Andante con larghezza, e fervente
mp
Oh like a queen's – her hap-py tread
poco rit.
L.H.
And like a queen's her gold-en head!
f – mf
But
oh! at last, when all is said, her wo-man's heart for me
calmato
p
We wand-ered where the riv – er gleamed
espress.
pp
espr

3.

p
'Neath oaks that mused and pines that dreamed A
p
mf
mf
wild thing of the woods she seemed, So proud, and pure, and free!
mf
poco più animato
All heav'n drew nigh to hear her sing When from her lips her
rit
p
a tempo primo.
mf
soul took wing The oaks for-got their pond-er-ing, The
p
sonoramente

4.
p
pines their rev-er - ie
ben cantando ma non troppo forte
p
estatico
And oh her hap - py queen-ly tread
poco slentando
a tempo
And oh her queen - ly gold-en head
But
con calore
oh her heart when all - is said
Her wo-man's heart
mf

5.
for
me
8va
allarg.
Poco pressanda
f
f
8va bassa
July 12/22.

Scene 6.
Where Loveliness keeps House
Madison Cawein.
R. Shepherd.
Andante placidamente
Here is the place where love-li-ness keeps house
Be-tween the riv-er and the wooded hills
With-in a val-ley where the spring-time spills her first-ling wind-flow'rs
poco cresc.

(A.S. Where loveliness ....) Seve 6-
2
mf
under blos-som-ing boughs
L.H.
p
mf
pp molto quieto
Where sum-mer sits braid ing her warm white brows with bramble roses; and where
ppp
legato
rit
a tempo
p
Aut - umn fills her lap with ast - ers
And old
mf
pp
Ped.
win t - er frills with crim - son haw and hip his snow - y blouse
mp

(A.S. Where loveliness..) Score G
3
pp
Here you may meet with Beau - ty Here
mf
she sits gaz ing up-on the moon or all the day
p
tun-ing a wood-thrush flute re - mote, un - seen
mf
(flautando)

(A.S. where loveliness..) Score G
4
Or when the storm is out
f strepitoso
più mosso
'Tis she who flits from
sub p scherzando
rock to rock a form of fly - ing spray
shout - ing, Be-neath the leaves' tu-mult - uous

5 (A.S. (Where loveliness . . .) Scene 6

Score I
Bacchus
Frank Dempster Sherman
A. Shepherd.
mp
List-en to the tawn-ey thief
Allegro leggermente
p
pp
Hid be-neath the wax-en leaf
mf
Growl — ing at his fair-y host
mf
Bid-ding her with ang-ry boast, Fill the cup with wine dis-tilled From the
pp
dew the dawn has spilled
mf
f

mf
Stored a - way in gold - en casks Is the prec - ious
p
draught he asks
mf
mp
Who, who makes this mim-ic din,
p
In this mim-ic meadow inn? Sings in such a drows - y
p

note
Wears a gold - en belt - ed coat
Loit — ers
in the daint-y room
Of this tav — ern of per —
— fume
Dares to ling - er - at the cup 'Till the
poco slentare
a tempo
pp
mf
p
mp

yel - low sun is up
Bac - chus 'tis come back a - gain To the
cresc.
Bus-y haunts of men
R.H.
L.H.
Garl-and-ed and gai-ly dressed

poco rit
mp rilassando
Bands of gold a - bout his breast,
Stray - ing from his Par - a - dise
p espress.
Hav - ing pin - ions an - gel - wise.
a tempo
p
f
'Tis the hon - ey bee who goes
mf
poco rit.
rev el-ing with-in the rose.
a tempo
p

mf
p
Jan. 1932

W. De La Mare
Reverie
R. Shepherd
♩= 108
Allegretto (with firm singing tone)
mf
mp
When slim So-
p
-phi-a mounts her horse And pac-es down the av-en-ue, It seems an in-ward
cantabile
mel-o-dy she pac-es to.
mp
Each

Reverie

2.
nar - row hoof is lift - ed high Be - neath the dark en - clustering pines
mp
A silv - er ray with - in his bit and brid - le shines
mf
mf
mf con intensità
His eye burns deep, his tail is arched and streams up - on the
p
shad - ow - y air, The day - light sleeks his jet - ty flanks, His
legato
Reverie

3.

p
mp
miss-tress' hair
Her hab - it flows in
espress.
p
mp
poco meno mosso
dark-ness down, Up - on the stirrup rests her foot, Her brow is lift-ed as if
earth she heed-ed not.
pp
'Tis sil-ent in the av-en-ue
pp
p
The somp-re pines are mute of song. The blue is dark, there moves no breeze the boughs a-mong.

Reverie

4.
poco rit
a tempo espress.
mf
mp
When slim So-phi-a mounts her horse And
pac-es down the av-en-ue, It seems an in-ward mel — o-dy she pac-es to.
poco a poco dim
rall. e dim. al fine
1932

Reverie

(see below) Score A
When Rooks fly Homeward
Seosamh MacCathmhaoil.
A. Shepherd.
Andte tranquillo
mf
When rooks fly
home-ward And shad - ows fall,
When ros-es fold on the hay-yard
wall,
When blind moths flut-ter By door - and tree,
Then comes the
mp
mf
p
pp
poco espress.
cresc.
(Reliable copy - but compare accompaniment with Score B - RNL)

mf
qui - et of Christ to me
con moto e semplice
p sempre legato
poco più mosso
p semplice
When stars look out on the
p sos.
child - ren's path
And gray mists gath - er on carn
— and rath
mp a tempo
pp poco trattenuto

3.
ben sostenuto ma ritmato
When night is one with the brood-ing sea
cresc. poco a poco
Then comes the qui-et of Christ to me
dim
molto dim.
espress.
Jan. 23rd, /41

Reverie (page 167) was, I believe, composed in C minor and later revised and transposed to B-flat minor. The copy that Shepherd gave me to photograph was the Shepherd Collection's Score E (B-flat minor), which is now missing. The RL process facsimile, the only record of Score E that I can find, appears here, which explains the poor quality of reproduction.

Reverie was published posthumously in C minor. If Shepherd authorized this key before his death it is, of course, definitive. However, knowing that the key of B-flat minor was once his preference, I have provided this version here.

When Rooks Fly Homeward (page 171). The two copies in the Shepherd Collection are different but seem equally reliable. On page 2, score 3, measure 4 of this version the pianist should play G-natural rather than G-sharp.

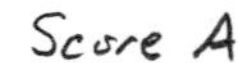

Sara Teasdale

April

R. Shepherd.

Andantino

mp

The roofs are shining from the rain, The sparrows twit-ter as they fly, And with the wind-y Ap-ril grace The lit-tle clouds go by.

Yet the back-yards are bare and brown With on-ly one un-changing

2.
mf
tree – I could not be so sure of Spring Save that it
mf
Sings in me
espressivo
Rit.
p
pp
Sept. 23, 1941

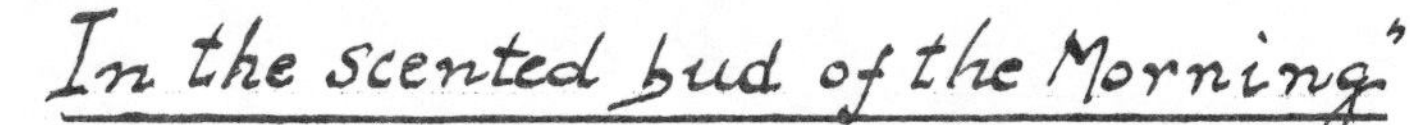

Score B

In the scented bud of the Morning

James Stephens

A. Shepherd.

Joyfully ♩. ± 96

mf *p* *mf* *f* *mp* *mf* *mp*

In the scent-ed bud of the morn-ing O, when the wind-y grass went ripp-ling far I saw my dear one walk-ing slow, In the field where the

L.H.

AS. In the Scented Dust. Score B
2
dais - ies are.
espress.
mp
We did not laugh and we did not
mf
speak As we wand - - ered hap-pi-ly to and fro
mf
I kissed my dear on eith - er cheek, In the

A.S. In the scented bud Score B

bud of the morn - ing O,

mf *f* Poco più animando

mf

A lark sang up from the breez - y land A lark sang down from a cloud a - far

p *mf* *p* *mf*

And

A.S. In the secluded bud Scene B.
4
mf
pp
p
she and I went hand in hand
In the
field where the dais- ies are.

Score E
Solitude
Harold Monro
A. Shepherd
Moderately slow
When you have tid-ied all things for the night, And while your thoughts are
sos. ped.
fad - ing to their sleep, You'll pause a mo-ment in the late fire-light
Too sor-row-ful to weep
poco più mosso
espress.

Shepherd, Solitude   Score
mp
The large and gent-le furn-i-ture has stood in
sym-pa-thet-ic si-lence all the day
mf
With that old kind-ness
poco rall.
a tempo
of do-mes-tic wood
poco più mosso
mf
Nev-er-the-less
mp
cresc.
The haunted room will say
f
'Some-one must be a-

Shepherd, Solitude Score E p. 3.
più mosso
p
- way
The lit - tle dog rolls ov - er half a -
Rit
p
pp
- wake
stretch - es his paws,
yawns,
looks up at you, Wags his
p
pochiss. accel.
mf atempo
tail ver - y
slight - ly for your sake that you may feel that he
is un - hap - py
too.
poco più mosso
mf
p
Allegretto
mp
A dist - ant en - gine whist - les, or the flloor creaks, or the
mf
p

Shepherd, Solitude, Scene E p.4.
Wand'ring night-wind bangs a door.
dim - e rit
Sil - ence is scat-tered like brok-en glass.
The min-utes prick their ears and run a - bout, then one by one sub-
- side a-gain and pass se-date-ly in, mo - not-on-ous-ly
poco rit.

Shepherd, Solitude Score E p 5
mf
teneramente
out.
You bend your head and
poco rit
p
wipe a-way a tear.
mf espress.
mf
mp
Sol - i-tude walks
One heav-y step
mp
pp
more near.
p sos. ped.
pp
ppp

The Charm (page 191) is a case similar to that above; two scores are necessary. This one is, I think, more reliable for the notes used, but the other would help with interpretation.

Heart's Journey (page 207). The problem is merely to decide if certain marks in two scores were made with Shepherd's approval. With the deaths of the principals I doubt that it is solvable.

Score A
Rowena Bennett.
Spring Duet
A. Shepherd
[Spring]
A - wake lit tle seed, a - wake and stir Out of the black earth's
mf
mp
sep - ul - chre .
Rise from the ground in a leaf - y tower, All the world is in
need of a flower .
[Wild Flower]
espress.
Why do you call to me? Why do you waken me
p

2.
You who come knocking with fin-gers of rain? Out of a beau-ti-ful dream you have shaken me
Let me go back to my slumb-er a-gain.
Rit.
[Spring]
a tempo
Hark, lit-tle seed, to the voice that calls! Burst through your roof top, tear down your walls.

3.
Earth may be coz-y, and qui-et and deep. But there's some-thing far better than dreaming and
poco rit
sleep, than dream-ing and sleep
[Wild flower]
Spring, is it you who are knocking and call-ing?
Help me to throw off this blanket of night!
mf

4.

Toss me a rope of your sun-shine to climb on That I may open my leaves to the
light
Jan. 16. 1942

Score B
The Charm
Thomas Campion
A. SHEPHERD
MUSIC COLL.
W.R.U. LIB.
R. Shepherd
Allegro mod^to. ♩ = 138
mf
Thrice toss these oak-en ash-es in the air, Thrice sit thou mute in this en-chant-ed chair, Then thrice three times tie up this true love's knot, And mur-mur soft, She will, or
Ped
mp
p
MSS
S548
E-3

mf
She will not
go
burn
these pois'nous
p
mf
weeds in yon blue
fire,
f
These
screech-owl's feath-ers
and this prick-ling brier
mf
mf
meno mosso
mp
This cyp-ress gath-ered at a
dead man's grave
p
poco più mosso
mf
That
all thy fears
and cares an end may have
poco slent.
mp

mf
Then come you fair - ies dance with me a round, Melt her hard
p
poco lent.
mp
espress.
heart with your mel - od - ious sound
legato
In
f meno mosso
vain, In vain are all the charms I can de - vise
poco
f

mf
She hath an art to break them with her eyes
pp
ah
f
accel. al fine.
f
f
'43

Score C
"Most quietly at times"
from the German of Cäsar Flaischlen
A. Shepherd
Molto tranquillo
Most qui-et-ly at times
and like a dream In thee re-ech-oes a far dist - ant song, Thou know-est not
whence suddenly it came. Thou know - est not what it would have of
thee
And like a dream most peace - ful-ly and still it dies in dist-ant

2.

mf
mus - ic ev-en as it came.
mf più animato
And sudden-ly, as in the crowd-ed street, or in the ver-y Winter's froz-en heart
p
mp
An od- our of ros-es will a-round thee breathe. Or as a pict-ure un-awares will
p
pp
pp
rise from far for-got-ten hap-py child-hood's days and gaze at thee, with eyes

3.
pp
in-quis-i-tive
pp
espress.
f con intensita
p
Most qui-et-ly and light-ly as a dream
pp
espress.
mf
Thou know-est not whence suddenly it came

4.
mf
Thou know-est not what it would have of thee.
p
And like a dream most peace-ful-ly and
still
it pales and pass-es
pp
fad-
-ing
whence it came
pp
pp
pp
ppp
8va
Aug. 23, 1943

Score B
The Truants
W. De La Mare
R. Shepherd
Andte. non troppo
Ere my heart beats too coldly and faintly To remember sad things yet be gay,
I would sing a brief song of the world's little children
poco rit.
Magic hath stolen away.
a tempo
The primroses scattered by April, The stars of the wide Milky way,
Cannot outnumber the hosts of the children Mag-

2.

mp
– ic hath stol-en a – way.
The butter-cup green of the meadows, The
snow of the blos-som-ing May,
Love – li – er are not than the legions of child-ren
Mag – ic hath stol-en a – way
Meno mosso
mf
The
Rit.
mf
Ped.
Ped.
waves toss-ing surf in the moon – beam,
The al-ba-tross lone on the

3.
ancora
Meno mosso
poco rit.
Spray A - lone Know the tears wept in vain for the child-ren Mag - ic hath
stol - en a - way
mf
ad lib.
In vain a -
tempo 1mo
mp
p
For at hush of the eve-ning, When the stars twinkle in-to the gray,
Seems to ech-o the far-a-way call-ing of child - ren
pp
espress.

4.
Mag - ic hath stol - en a - way.
senza rit.
p
pp
Jan. 30, 1945

WRU Score D
Ok.
Matin Song
Thomas Heywood
(1575 - 1650)
R. Shepherd.
Allegro giocoso
♩= 116
Pack clouds a - way! and wel-come day With night we ban - ish sor-row. Sweet air, blow soft; mount, lark, a-loft, to give my Love good-mor-row! Wings from the wind to please her mind, Notes
ten.
a tempo
Ped.
34.4

2.
poco meno mosso
mp
from the lark I'll bor-row.
Bird prune thy wing! Night-in-gale
sing! To give my Love good-morrow!
a tempo
mf
To give my Love good-
-mor-row Notes from them all I'll bor-row.
mf
mf
mp
mf
mf
p poco rit
più animato
♩ = 168
mf
Wake from thy nest Rob-in red-breast
mf
p

3.
Sing birds in ev'ry fur-row, And from each hill let mus-ic shrill
give my love good-mor-row
rit.
meno mosso
Black-bird and thrush in ev-'ry bush, stare, lin-net and
8va
mf
p
Cock sparrow!
You pretty elves a-mong your
mp

4.
poco rilassare
a tempo
-selves
Sing my fair love good - mor-row-
mf
p
pochiss. alarg.
f
To give my Love good-mor row!
mf
L.H.
Sing birds in ev' — ry furrow!
a tempo
f
8va
8va
f
Feb. 27, 1948

Heart's Journey
Siegfried Sassoon
R. Shepherd
Andantino
cresc.
Song
Be my soul
set forth the fairest
part Of all that moved har-mon - ious through my heart;
And
gather me to your arms
mp teneramente
for we must go to child-hood's

gar-den, to child-hood's gar-den when the moon is low
pp
And ov-er the leaf shadow lat-ticed grass the whispering wraiths of my
mf
mp
dead selves re-pass.
p
rall.
a tempo
pp
mf
mf
Soul
f
dim.

legg.
poco tratt.
a tempo
p
be my song; re-turn ar-rayed in white; Lead
dim.
pp
mp
mf
cresc.
f
home the loves that I have wronged and slain
mf
cresc.
più agitato
con intensità
f
ff
rilassare
rall. e dim
a tempo e con anima
poco cresc.
Bring back the sum - mer dawns that
mp

ban-ished night With dist-ant-warbling bird notes aft-er rain
mp a tempo
ppp
Time's way worn
poco rit.
trav-el-ler I. And you,
legg.
Sempre p
pp
ppp
O
Song, and you O
poco cresc.
mf
sub p

Soul
O soul, my Par-a-dise laid waste
So
sempre legg.
p
pp
long.
poco rall.
trang.
mf
mp
espress.
pochiss.
dim.
p
pp
Aug. 16, 1955

SPINNING SONG
Edith Sitwell
Arthur Shepherd
Moderato ♩=80
mf
f
con sordino
mp
mf
pp
The mil- ler's
daugh- ter Combs her hair,
Like flocks of doves As soft as

vair..
Oh, how those soft flocks flut- ter
down Ov— er the emp- ty grass- y town.
p

senza sordino
mf espress.
mf
Like a queen in a crown of gold light, she sits 'neath the
mp Più mosso 𝅗𝅥=92
p
mf
f
shad- ows' flick-er-ing tree—
p
Till the old dame went the
pp
p
pizz.
f
way she came, Play-ing bob-cherr-y with a can-dle-flame.

* Speaking voice begins after the fermata.

legg.
p
mf
p
'Not a crumb,' said Min, 'To a mouse I'll be giv-ing, For a mouse must spin To earn her liv-ing'. So poor Mrs.
pizz.
arco
colla parte
f
cresc.

pizz.
f
Mouse and her three cross Aunts nib-ble snow that rus-tles like
arco
sulpont.
mf
gold wheat plants.
poco accel.
cresc.
rit.
p
mf
P
And the mil-ler's daugh-ter combs her
rit.
pp

liberamente
mp
a tempo
locks. Like run- ning wa- ter Those dove-soft flocks;
P
And her
mouth is sweet as a hon- ey-flow- er cold,
But her
heart is heav- y as bags of gold.
8va
pp

8
liberamente
tr
ten.
tr
mf
12
The shad-ow mice said,
8va
pp
mf
a tempo
3
We will line with down From those
p legato
doves, our bed And our slip- pers and down, For

mp
ev'- ry - thing comes to the shad - ows at last
If the spin - ning - wheel Time move
rall.
slow or fast?
a tempo
p

poco accel.
pizz.
f
p

Score B
Sarasvati
James Stephens
R. Shepherd.
At moderate pace
mf
As bird to nest, when mood-i-ly the
Storm- cloud mur-murs nigh the tree.
poco cresc.
Thus let him flee
who can to sing,
Here hath he calm and shelt-er-ing.
cresc.

A.S. Sarasvati Score B

2

A.S. Sarasvati Scene B
run-ning where the thund-er shudders through the air,
Thus
let him flee who can to sing,
rit.
teneramente
Here hath he ward and
cher - ish - ing.
espress.
poco trattenuto e con chiarezza
a tempo
accel.
Fly to thy tal-ent, To thy charm, Thy nest

A.S. Sarasvati Score B
4
thine hive, thy shelt-er-ing arm, Who
can to sing,
There let him
flee, This is, naught else is
cer- tain-ty.
Oct. 4, 1957

CLASSIFIED LIST OF ARTHUR SHEPHERD'S WORKS

APPENDIX A

Works for which no publisher is indicated are in manuscript. The asterisks (*) indicate that facsimiles are reproduced in this volume. This list is drawn from a number of sources: the Arthur Shepherd Collection (see below), Shepherd's own compilations and lists of his works, William S. Newman's list in his article "Arthur Shepherd" (*Musical Quarterly* 36 [April 1950]: 159*ff*), and miscellaneous references in letters and other sources. Not all dates are confirmed; some are from scores, others are dates of publication or first performance. Shepherd was not consistent in titling or referring to his works, either from score to score, from score to performance, or from year to year. When more than one title is given the first is the one Shepherd preferred in his later years; exceptions are noted. Titles that appear on a manuscript score or published copy are italicized. Note that in a few cases Shepherd habitually used a different title from that under which the work was published. The authors of the texts of choral works and songs are listed in Appendix B.

Arthur Shepherd possessed copies of most of his works. His manuscripts and personal copies of published compositions are now housed in the Arthur Shepherd Collection in the Marriott Library of Fine Arts of the University of Utah in Salt Lake City, which has published a good catalogue. It also possesses the larger, descriptive card catalogue that I prepared for the Freiberger Library (see page 47) in 1958, in which the various scores and versions of each work (often there are several) are identified. For many compositions I was able to indicate which scores are preferable or probably definitive. Whenever publication, recording, or an important performance of one of Shepherd's manuscript works is undertaken, the catalogue should be consulted and the various scores compared side by side in order that the best version may be used. In this list the lost manuscripts are indicated by a dagger (†).

ORCHESTRAL WORKS

?	†Overture, *The Nuptials of Attila.*
?	*Marche pittoresque et scene orientale* (Op. 5d).
?	*Marsyas (Symphonic Idyll).*
?	†*The Twelve Days of Christmas.* Parts only.
1901	(1) *Overture Joyeuse;* (2) *A Joyful Overture* (Op. 3; this score dated June 1905).
1915	(1) Overture, The Festival of Youth; (2) *The Festival of Youth.*
1916	(1) Fantasie for Piano and Orchestra; (2) *Fantasie Humoreske for Piano and Orchestra;* (3) *Humoresque;* (4) *Fantasie.* Dedicated to Heinrich Gebhard.
ca. 1918	*Marche Solonelle.* Written for military band. Later revised for orchestra.
1919	*Overture to a Drama.* Boston: C. C. Birchard & Co., 1925. Dedicated to Nikolai Sokoloff.
1927	(1) Horizons, Symphony No. 1; (2) *Horizons, Four Western Pieces for Symphony Orchestra.* Boston: C. C. Birchard & Co. for the Juilliard Musical Foundation, 1929; (3) Nature Symphony. Dedicated "To my wife."

1930 *Choreographic Suite on an Exotic Theme.* See "Piano Music: 1928, *Exotic Dance*" below.

1932 *Sinfonia Domestica di Famiglia Blossom.*

1938 *Symphony No. 2.*

1942 *"Hilaritas," Overture for Concert Band.* Dedicated to Arthur Williams and the Oberlin Concert Band.

1943 (1) *Fantasia Concertante on "The Garden Hymn;"* (2) *Fantasia on "The Garden Hymn."* See under organ works.

1946 (1) *Fantasy Overture on Down East Spirituals;* (2) *Fantasia on Down East Spirituals.*

Concerto for Violin and Orchestra.

1952 (1) *Variations on an Original Theme* (title on late scores); (2) *Theme and Variations* (title of program of first performance. Preference seems optional); (3) *Theme and Variations for Orchestra.* Dedicated to George Szell and the Cleveland Orchestra.

CHORAL WORKS

1907 *The Lord Hath Brought Again Zion.* Mixed voices (SATB div.) and baritone solo with orchestra or organ. Vocal score: Boston: Oliver Ditson Co., 1907; orchestral manuscript dated 1925.

1913 *The City in the Sea.* Cantata for double chorus, baritone solo, and orchestra. Vocal score: Boston: The Boston Music Co., 1913. Dedicated "To my dear Mother."

1914 Sergei Rachmaninoff. *Glorious Forever.* Arranged by Arthur Shepherd for mixed voices (SATTB) with piano. Boston: Boston Music Co., 1914.

1915 *Song of the Sea Wind.* Women's voices (SSA) and orchestra or piano. Vocal score: Boston: Arthur P. Schmidt Co., 1915.

He Came All So Still. Women's voices (SSAA) with piano. Boston: Arthur P. Schmidt, Co., 1915. See also "Songs: ca. 1950."

1918 *O Jesu, Who Art Gone Before.* Anthem, mixed voices (SATB) and baritone solo with organ. Boston: Boston Music Co., 1921.

Deck Thyself My Soul. Communion Hymn, mixed voices (SATB), organ ad lib. Boston: Boston Music Co., 1921.

1931 *Comrades.* Men's voices (TTBB) with piano.

G. F. Handel. "The Lord Shall Reign" from *Israel in Egypt.* Arranged for double chorus of men's voices (TTBB/TTBB) with piano by Arthur Shepherd. Accompaniment adapted from the version of Mendelssohn. London: Oxford University Press, 1931.

1932 *The Song of the Pilgrims.* Cantata for double chorus, tenor solo, and orchestra. Vocal score: Boston: C. C. Birchard & Co., 1937. Dedicated to Percy Goetschius.

1934 *A Ballad of Trees and the Master.* Mixed voices (SAATTBB), a cappella. Boston: C. C. Birchard & Co., 1935.

1936 *Invitation to the Dance.* Mixed voices (SATB) with orchestra or two pianos. Vocal score (Ozalid process): Claremont, Calif. Richard N. Loucks, 1955. Dedicated to James Aliferis. Copyright 1955 by Arthur Shepherd.

1938 *Grace for Gardens.* Mixed voices (SSATB), a cappella. New York: Arrow Music Press, Inc., 1939.

Build Thee More Stately Mansions. Mixed voices (SATB) and organ or piano. (Withdrawn. See under "Songs: 1938 *The Chambered Nautilus.*")

1939 *A Prayer in Spring.* Mixed voices (SSATTB), or men's voices (TTBB), a cappella (piano reduction on one score presumably for rehearsal only).

1940 *Carol.* Soprano, alto, and piano. Published privately as a Christmas card in 1940. New York: Music Press, Inc., 1947.

1941 *Planting a Tree.* Mixed voices (SATB), probably a cappella (piano accompaniment on one manuscript probably intended for rehearsal only).

Slowly, Silently Now the Moon. Women's voices (SSA) and piano.

In the Cool of the Evening. Men's voices (TTBB), a cappella.

Jolly Wat (Canticum Nativitatis Christi). Two equal voices (solo or chorus) and orchestra or piano. Vocal score: New York: Music Press, 1947.

Ye Mariners of England. Men's voices (TTBB div.) and piano or orchestra. Vocal score: New York: Boosey & Co. (Boosey, Hawkes, Belwin), 1941.

1944 *Psalm XLII.* Quartet, chorus (SATB div.), and orchestra or organ. Vocal score: Boston: C. C. Birchard & Co., 1950. Dedicated "To my dear Mother."

1947 *Drive On!* Mixed chorus (SATB), with baritone solo and orchestra or piano. Vocal score: Boston: C. C. Birchard & Co., 1947.

1951 *The Word.* Mixed voices (SATB div.) with organ. Boston: C. C. Birchard & Co., 1951. Dedicated to the Alumni Association of the New England Conservatory of Music.

1956 *A Psalm of the Mountains.* Mixed voices (SATB) with orchestra or piano.

CHAMBER MUSIC

1905 †Two Movements for String Quartet

ca. 1916–20 (1) Sonata for Pianoforte and Violin; (2) *Sonata pour violon et piano.* Paris: Editions Maurice Senart, 1927.

[Note: When I knew him Shepherd was no longer certain about the date of the Violin Sonata. His mimeographed catalogue gives 1927 as the year of publication. William S. Newman's catalogue ("Arthur Shepherd," *The Musical Quarterly* 36 (April 1950): 159 ff.) lists the date of composition as between 1916 and 1920. I have adopted this date in my catalogue, thinking that Newman may have had information unavailable to me. Claire Reis ("Arthur Shepherd," *Composers in America*) gives 1924. The earliest evidence of its existence that I have been able to find is a performance at the Cleveland Museum of Art by Arthur Shepherd and Arthur Beckwith in 1924.]

1925 (1) *Triptych for High Voice and String Quartet.* New York: G. Schirmer for the Society for the Publication of American Music, 1927. (There are two editions, the second slightly revised.) (2) *Three Songs from "Gitanjali."* (3) *Triptych for Soprano and String Quartet,* title of the Kraft/Walden recording. Dedicated to Adella Prentiss Hughes.

1926 (1) *Quartet;* (2) *Quartet No. 1a;* (3) String Quartet in G Minor, 1926.

1933 *Quartet for Strings in E Minor.* New York: J. Fischer & Bros. for the Society for the Publication of American Music, 1935. In his later years Shepherd considered this to be his First Quartet. Dedicated to the Cleveland String Quartet: Josef Fuchs, Rudolph Ringwall, Carlton Cooley, Victor de Gómez.

1936 *Quartet for Strings No. 2.* D Minor. Commissioned in 1935 by The League of Composers.

1940 (1) *Quintet for Pianoforte and Strings;* (2) *Quintet for Piano and Strings.* Dedicated to the Walden String Quartet: Homer Schmitt, Bernard Goodman, Leroy Collins, Robert Swenson.

1942 *Praeludium Salutatorium for Divers Instruments.* Flute, oboe, horn, bassoon, violin, viola, cello. Commissioned for the 25th anniversary of the League of Composers.

1943 (1) *Divertissement for Quintet of Wind Instruments;* (2) *Divertissement for Flute, Oboe, Clarinet, Horn, Bassoon* (probably withdrawn).

1944 *Quartet for Strings No. 3.* D Minor.

1955 *Quartet for Strings No. 4.* C Major.

PIANO MUSIC

? *Pantomime Chinois.*

1895–96 Student Compositions:
Scherzo.
Romanza for the Pianoforte. Boston: New England Conservatory Quarterly, 1896. Microfilm copy obtainable from the Library of Congress.

1900 *Waltz.*

1903? *Theme and Variations.* Newton Center, Mass.: The Wa-Wan Press, 1903 (?).
Intermezzo.

1904 *Etude.*
Capriccio.

1905 *Mazurka* (op. 2, no. 1). Newton Center, Mass.: The Wa-Wan Press, 1905. Dedicated to Miss Hattie Jennings.

	**Prelude* (op. 2, no. 2). Newton Center, Mass.: The Wa-Wan Press, ca. 1905.
1907	(1) *Sonata for the Pianoforte,* Op. 4. Boston: Boston Music Co., 1911. (2) *Sonata No. 1;* (3) *Sonata in F Minor.*
1908	*Nocturn.* B Minor.
1920	*Fugue for the Pianoforte in C-Sharp Minor.**
1920?	†*From a Mountain Lake.*
1922	*Fugue for the Pianoforte in C Minor.*
1928	*Exotic Dance.* New York: Oxford University Press, 1930. This work is the basis of the orchestral work, *Choreographic Suite on an Exotic Theme.*
	Nocturn. C Major.
1930	*Second Sonata.* New York: Oxford University Press, 1930; 2d ed. 1951. Dedicated to Beryl Rubinstein.
1931	*Prelude.** B-flat Minor.
	Gigue Fantasque. Bryn Mawr, Penn.: Theodore Presser Co., 1956. Dedicated "To my brother, Charles."
	*Eclogue No. 1.**
1932	*Prelude.** G Minor.
1935	*Autumn Fields.* New York: Carl Fischer, Inc., 1936.
	Gay Promenade. New York: Carl Fischer, Inc., 1936.
1938	*Lento Amabile.* Bryn Mawr, Penn.: Theodore Presser Co., 1956. Dedicated to Noble Kreider.
	(1) *Capriccio No. 1** (rev. 1941); (2) *Capriccio I;* (3) *Capriccio.*
	Intermezzo.
1939	*Two Step.**
1941	(1) *Nocturne;** (2) *Nocturne No. 2.* F Minor.
	Exotic Dance II.
	(1) *Exotic Dance No. 3* (rev. 1954); (2, *Exotic Dance III.*
	Capriccio II. New York: G. Ricordi, 1954. Dedicated to Vivien Harvey.
1943	*Scherzino.**
	*Capriccio No. 3.**
1945	(1) *In Modo Ostinato.* Bryn Mawr, Penn.: Theodore Presser Co., 1956; (2) *Rustic Ramble.*
	*Souvenir.** Dedicated to G. P. S. [Grazella P. Shepherd].
1947	*Badinage.* Several revisions; apparently none satisfactory to Shepherd.
1948	(1) *Processionale Festivo**; (2) *Dance Episode* (title discarded).
	Dance Episode. (Apparently withdrawn. One copy dedicated to Kalman Novak.)
	(1) *Eclogue No. 2;* (2) *Eclogue No. 2, Primavera.*
	(1) *Eclogue.* Bryn Mawr, Penn.: Theodore Presser Co., 1956; (2) *Eclogue No. 4, Summer Reverie.*
1949	*Eclogue No. 3.**

ORGAN MUSIC

?	*Processionale.*
1904?	†*Prelude in B Minor.*
1912	*Prelude and Fugue in E Minor.*
1923	*Prelude.* E Minor.
1939	*Fantasia on "The Garden Hymn."* New York: H. W. Gray Co., 1940. See orchestral works. Dedicated to Arthur Quimby.

SONGS

Except as otherwise noted, these works have an accompaniment for piano.

?	*Evening Song.*
	I Dreamt of a Monarch's Daughter Fair.
1895	Student Compositions:
	†*Daybreak.*
	†*The Sabbath of the Soul.*
1901	*Oh, There's a King.*
1905	†*Wanderlust.*
	†*The Desert.*
1906	†*A Star in the Night.*
1908	*Youth's Spring Tribute.*
1909	*Five Songs on Poems of James Russell Lowell.* Op. 7. Newton Center, Mass.: The Wa-Wan Press, 1909.
	No. 1. †*Lift Up the Curtains of Thine Eyes* (1907).
	No. 2. *Nocturn* (1907). Holograph score in Library of Congress.
	No. 3. *There Is a Light in Thy Blue Eyes* (1907).
	No. 4. *The Lost Child* (1908).
	No. 5. *Rhapsody* (1908).
ca. 1909?	*Sun Down.** Dedicated to Miss Edna C. Cohn.
1912	*Sunday up the River.**
1915	*The Gentle Lady** in *The Art of Music,* vol. 4. New York: The National Society of Music, 1916. Dedicated "To my sister, Josephine."
1921	*The Little Stream.*
1922	*Oh, Like a Queen's Her Happy Tread.**

1931 *Where Loveliness Keeps House.**

1932 *The Fiddlers.* South Hadley, Mass., Mt. Holyoke College and Northampton, Mass., Smith College: The Valley Music Press, 1948. Dedicated to Marie Simmelink Kraft.

*Bacchus.** Dedicated to Marie Simmelink Kraft.

Softly Along the Road of Evening. South Hadley, Mass., Mt. Holyoke College and Northampton, Mass., Smith College: The Valley Music Press, 1961.

*Reverie.** South Hadley, Mass., Mt. Holyoke College and Northampton, Mass., Smith College: The Valley Music Press, 1961.

1937 *Golden Stockings.* South Hadley, Mass., Mt. Holyoke College and Northampton, Mass., Smith College: The Valley Music Press, 1961. Dedicated to Marguerite Quimby.

1938 *The Chambered Nautilus.* (The text is verse five of Oliver Wendell Holmes's poem. The score is undated, but seems musically related to the withdrawn choral work, *Build Thee More Stately Mansions,* which sets verse six of the same poem. These two are possibly fragments of a larger unfinished work.)

1941 *When Rooks Fly Homeward.**

*April.**

(1) *To a Trout.* South Hadley, Mass., Mt. Holyoke College and Northampton, Mass., Smith College: The Valley Music Press, 1961. (2) *The Trout.*

*In the Scented Bud of the Morning.**

Virgil. South Hadley, Mass., Mt. Holyoke College and Northampton, Mass., Smith College: The Valley Music Press, 1961. Dedicated "To the memory of Charles Martin Loeffler."

*Solitude.**

1942 *Spring Duet.**

1943 *The Charm.**

*Most Quietly at Times.**

1944 *The Starling Lake.* South Hadley, Mass., Mt. Holyoke College and Northampton, Mass., Smith College: The Valley Music Press, 1948. Dedicated to Marie Simmelink Kraft.

1945 *The Truants.**

1948 *Matin Song.**

1949 *Spinning Song,** for voice, piano, and viola. Dedicated to Gretchen Garnett and Muriel Carmen.

Serenade, for voice, piano, and viola. South Hadley, Mass., Mt. Holyoke College and Northampton, Mass., Smith College: The Valley Music Press, 1961.

ca. 1950 *He Came All So Still.** Arrangement of the choral work of the same title.

1951 *Morning Glory.* South Hadley, Mass., Mt. Holyoke College and Northampton, Mass., Smith College: The Valley Music Press, 1961.

1955 *Heart's Journey.**

1957 *Sarasvati.**

SONGS WITH ENSEMBLE OR ORCHESTRAL ACCOMPANIMENT

1925 *Triptych.* See under "Chamber Music."

1931 *Where Loveliness Keeps House.* See under "Songs." Accompaniment for symphony orchestra; date unknown.

1932 *Bacchus.* See under "Songs." Accompaniment for symphony orchestra less trombones and tuba; date unknown.

The Fiddlers. See under "Songs." Accompaniment for nine string players.

Softly Along the Road of Evening. See under "Songs." Accompaniment for an orchestra of strings, woodwinds, and horns; date unknown.

RECORDINGS

Triptych for Soprano (sic) *and String Quartet.* Marie Simmelink Kraft, soprano; The Walden String Quartet. The American Recording Society. No. ARS-18, ca. 1948.

Songs of Arthur Shepherd. Marie Simmelink Kraft, mezzo-soprano; Marianne Matousek Mastics, piano. Published by the Department of Music of Western Reserve University, ca. 1960.

Piano Music of Arthur Shepherd. Vivien Harvey Slater, pianist. Published by the Department of Music of Western Reserve University. Copyright 1967.

Triptych for High Voice and String Quartet. Betsy Norden, soprano; The Emerson String Quartet. New World Records. No. NW218, 1977.

Sonata for Pianoforte and Violin, in the album *A Cleveland Heritage.* David Cerone, violin; Grant Johannesen, piano. Cleveland Institute of Music Series, distributed by Golden Crest Records, Inc., 220 Broadway, Huntington Station, NY 11746; ca. 1977.

BOOKS, ARTICLES, AND LECTURES

Articles published by the Music Supervisors National Conference and the Music Teachers National Association were delivered as lectures at conventions of those organizations. Works without bibliographical ascriptions are typed or handwritten copies in the Shepherd Collection. Many of the latter are undated, and some may have been classroom lectures.

"Adventures in Music Analysis." Unfinished book manuscript. 1927–28.

"American Music in the Limelight." *Volume of Proceedings of the Music Teachers National Association* 41 (1947): 33–37.

"American Music, or Music in America." Lecture. No date.

"American Music: the Traditionalists." Lecture No. 1. 1939.

"American Orchestral Music, 1900–1950." *Volume of Proceedings of the Music Teachers National Association* 44 (1950): 1–10.

"American Violin Music since 1876." *Volume of Proceedings of the Music Teachers National Association* 23 (1928): 220–26.

"Attitudes and Responses: Lecture for Ohio Music Teachers." No date.

"Berlioz." Lecture at Institute of Music. No date.

"Biographical Sketch."

"The Cadence in the Music of J. S. Bach." *Volume of Proceedings of the Music Teachers National Association* 29 (1934): 188–208.

"Church Music." Lecture No. 2. No date.

"Cleveland." In G. C. Sansoni, ed., *Enciclopedia dello spettacolo.* 9 vols. Rome: Casa Editrice le Maschere, 1956. Vol. 3, cols. 973–78. [Shepherd's original text is in English; the manuscript is in the Shepherd Collection.]

Cobbett, Walter Willson. *Cobbett's Cyclopedic Survey of Chamber Music.* 2 vols. London: Oxford University Press, 1929; 2d ed. (3 vols.). Edited by Colin Mason. London: Oxford University Press, 1963. [Arthur Shepherd contributed the articles on Frederic Ayres, Mrs. H. H. A. Beach, Frederick Shepherd Converse, Carl Engel, Rubin Goldmark, Henry Hadley, William Clifford Heilman, Henry Holden Huss, Edgar Stillman Kelley, Daniel Gregory Mason, and David Stanley Smith.]

"Commencement Address, Longy School of Music." 13 June 1950.

"Fashions, Survivals, and Vitality in Music: or, The Goings On and Happenings in Music." Museum lecture. 1 March 1954.

"Harmonic Values—an Inquiry." *Volume of Proceedings of the Music Teachers National Association* 5 (1910): 115–23.

"Haydn." Lecture at Institute of Music. 1941.

"Listening In on the Masters." Alice Keith and Arthur Shepherd. Cleveland, Ohio: Cleveland Public Schools, 1926.

"Music as a Vocation." Radio talk over WTAM. 14 April 1931.

"Music in Higher Education." Lecture. 1936–37.

"Music in My Time." Lecture at the University of Illinois. 15 November 1955.

"On Methods of Analytical Study of American Music." Lecture. No date.

"Orchestral Concerts for Children." *Journal of Proceedings of the Music Supervisors' National Conference* 16 (1923): 113–15.

"Papa Goetschius in Retrospect." *The Musical Quarterly* 30, no. 3 (July 1944): 307–18.

"Cleveland Orchestra Program Notes." Third through twelfth seasons (1920–30). Huntington Library, San Marino, California.

"Purcell." Lecture at Institute of Music. 1940.

"Schubert." Lecture at Institute of Music. No date.

"Schumann." Lecture at Institute of Music. 10 December 1937.

The String Quartets of Ludwig van Beethoven: Historic and Analytic Commentaries. Cleveland, Ohio: Horace Carr, 1935. [Dedicated "In remembrance of Anna Creighton Higgins."]

"Types of Non-Professional Offerings." *Journal of Proceedings of the Music Supervisors' National Conference* 25 (1932): 194–97.

"Wit in Music." Lecture. No date.

MISCELLANEOUS

The Shepherd Collection contains the correspondence of Arthur Shepherd, including most of the letters referred to in this book. In addition, twenty-four sketchbooks are preserved in the Shepherd Collection. These contain sketches for many of the works listed above, as well as unidentified sketches, exercises, aphorisms, addresses, and notes of all kinds. Also in the Shepherd Collection are eighteen books of various kinds of teaching materials, including more sketches, figured basses, harmony exercises, counterpoints, twelve-tone exercises, class lists, class notes and lesson plans, and the other records of a classroom professor of music.

ARTHUR SHEPHERD'S POETS

APPENDIX B

Songs and choral works are arranged according to the authors of the texts. The titles are those of the musical compositions and are not always identical with the titles of the poems. For those marked with an asterisk (*), facsimile manuscripts can be found in Part 3.

Allen, Florence Ellinwood	*A Psalm of the Mountains*
Anonymous or undetermined	*A Star in the Night* *He Came All So Still** (carol) *The Desert* *The Sabbath of the Soul* *Wanderlust*
Apollinaris, Sidonius (trans. Howard Mumford Jones)	*Invitation to the Dance*
Bennett, Rowena	*Spring Duet**
Brooke, Rupert	*The Song of the Pilgrims*
Campbell, Thomas	*Ye Mariners of England*
Campion, Thomas	*The Charm**
Carman, Bliss	*The City in the Sea*
Cawein, Madison	*Where Loveliness Keeps House**
Chandler, J. (trans. from the Latin)	*O Jesu, Who Art Gone Before*
De La Mare, Walter	*The Fiddlers* *Reverie** *Softly Along the Road of Evening* *Slowly, Silently Now the Moon* *The Truants**
Doctrine and Covenants (volume of Mormon scripture)	*The Lord Hath Brought Again Zion*
Driscoll, Louise	*Grace for Gardens*
Flaischlen, Cäsar (trans. Jethro Bithell)	*Most Quietly at Times**
Franck, Johann	*Deck Thyself My Soul*
Frost, Robert	*A Prayer in Spring*
Goethe, Johann Wolfgang von	*Evening Song*
Gogarty, Oliver St. John	*Golden Stockings* *To a Trout* *Virgil*
Heine, Heinrich	*I Dreamt of a Monarch's Daughter Fair* *Oh, There's a King*
Henley, William Ernest	*Sun Down**
Heywood, Thomas	*Matin Song**
Hill, Richard	*Carol* *Jolly Wat*
Holmes, Oliver Wendell	*The Chambered Nautilus* *Build Thee More Stately Mansions* (from *The Chambered Nautilus*)
Hovey, Richard	*Comrades*
Lanier, Sidney	*A Ballad of Trees and the Master*
Longfellow, Henry Wadsworth	*Daybreak*
Lowell, James Russell	*Lift Up the Curtains of Thine Eyes* *Nocturn* *There is a Light in Thy Blue Eyes*

	The Lost Child
	Rhapsody
Mac Cathmhaoil, Seosamh (Joseph Campbell)	*When Rooks Fly Homeward**
Masefield, John	*The Gentle Lady**
Merit, Gary	*Drive On!*
Monro, Harold	*Solitude**
Nekrásof, Aleksyévitch (trans. Nathan Haskell Dole)	*Glorious Forever*
Noyes, Alfred	*In the Cool of the Evening*
O'Sullivan, Seumas	*The Starling Lake*
Psalm 42	
Rossetti, Dante Gabriel	*Youth's Spring Tribute*
Sassoon, Siegfried	*Heart's Journey**
	Morning Glory
Sharp, William (Fiora Macleod)	*Song of the Sea Wind*
Shepherd, Richard	*The Little Stream*
Sherman, Frank Dempster	*Bacchus**
Sitwell, Sacheverel	*Serenade*
Sitwell, Edith	*Spinning Song**
Stephens, James	*In the Scented Bud of the Morning**
	*Sarasvati**
Tagore, Rabindranath	*Triptych:* "He It Is"; "The Day Is No More"; "Light, My Light."
Teasdale, Sara	*April**
Thomson, James (Bysshe Vanolis)	*Sunday up the River**
Tourjee, Eben	*The Word*
Turner, Nancy Byrd	*Planting a Tree*
Watson, William	*Oh, Like a Queen's Her Happy Tread**

LETTERS FROM ARTHUR FARWELL

APPENDIX C

2 Oct 07

Dear Shepherd—

As to intellect and composition—of course no man can have *too* great an intellect—the more the merrier. The question is—what to *do* with an intellect. One mustn't carry the doing of "stunts" to the point where it overbalances the sense of beauty, as I feel that you sometimes do. It seems to me that you too often get to the point where your music is interesting rather than lovable. Yet the limitation there may be in *me,* in lack of the proper perception. Yet I have experienced a good deal, and respond pretty broadly. It seems to me that you express a very restless spirit—which ought to be balanced somehow by the great deeps of peace. Perhaps you are not familiar with the latter! I am wondering what the slow movement of your Sonata [possibly the *Sonata for the Pianoforte,* Op. 4] is like. I like the Sonata—what I have heard of it, better, I think, than anything else I know of yours.

Perhaps you will work through a certain dryness I feel in your music, which may be chiefly your closeness to the "academics," and express a more juicy, a more musical self, as your intellect gets to dealing more and more with what is truly your *own* spirit. I feel that your music is more a science than an art at present. You've got to bring your faculty of art-intoxication up to your capacity for thought,—at least that is as it seems to me. There are many ways of doing that, each artist must have his own. For some it's literature, for some it's other music than their own, for some nature, etc. It seems to me that you've got to strike a compromise, and take off some of the thought you are now putting into harmony and form, and apply it to melody and to the more accurate interpretation of unified mood. Mood, as a *master,* has killed many modern artists,—but it is a most invaluable servant, and must be at one's command. There are so many different things going on, and following each other in rapid succession in your music that you don't throw the hearer into a dream, enchant him as a magician (i.e., a musician) should, but shake him up and rattle him round and discomfort him. Now it's a power to be able to do that, but in the large scope of musical expression, that is but one power. With *me* as critic, express one single compelling uninterrupted unit *mood,* instead of a rapid series of interesting harmonic and thematic stunts.

Keep all the intellect you have or can get, by all means,—but open it to all the necessary elements, divide its application in proper ratio, and don't let it harden in a certain direction alone.

Take this for what it's worth.

* * *

Address Newton Center
(though I'm at Auburn
N.Y. now)

Nov. 20 [probably 1907]

Dear Shepherd,

You have written me that a change is necessary in your life—that you will leave Salt Lake, and that you want to go East.

The *need* of a big change lies before me too. Can we not find a solution of it all in helping each other?

The Wa-Wan Society is working out well, is the *realest* thing I have undertaken yet, because the most immediately *human,* and is the only pathway being cleared for the broad, national, systematic hearing of American composers' work. There are now six Centers, since Rochester and Buffalo are added, and others are to follow. Here is a little practical grip, little enough in extent, but big with significance. Let this work be pushed further, let Center after Center be organized—it's not so very difficult—and soon enough we will have a great force in motion—a force that must be reckoned with in the development of American music, a force second to no other, in extent, and in intelligently directed effort. Wherever this work touches, it reaches and unites the best elements in the community.

There will be fallings away, siftings, and disloyalties—as are always the case—but the dead may bury their dead, and we soon discover the faithful, and find our normal and rightful following.

As you will [this word may be *well*] know, it is no whim, but deep *Need,* that has driven me into this work—need of a place in American life for an American composer, as a *composer;* not only as a teacher or a player. And need of a practical work which should also satisfy this need. It has all led, little as I foresaw it, to the Wa-Wan Society—there is the creating of the necessary condition for advance as a composer, and there is a practical work, by means of which we can step to that condition.

This *need* that I speak of I do not feel to be a personal thing. I believe only that I am the first one to feel it with sufficient intensity to act upon it, and that in doing so, I am responding to a need arising in many others, however much or little its full force has yet dawned upon them. It must dawn upon them with ever-increasing intensity, as composers begin to realize fully that they are Americans after all, living in America, and that Europe is going to give them nothing but traditions of artistic heroism, and occasional contemporary inspirations. Our life, our home is here! Therefore we must, in our need, make it acceptable, desirable, to us, as composers.

The Wa-Wan Society, aiming directly at the satisfying of this need, will be a power in our hands exactly in proportion as we extend its organization. And if I can do as much as I can alone, burdened also with other tasks, how rapidly and strongly we could bring it forward, did but several of us unite and act concertedly. It would give it a tremendous impetus, in name, and practical results.

In regard to the latter; this month I have done work in organizing, which will bring in about five hundred dollars, one half of which is profit—and a good deal of the time I have been laying off, visiting and doing literary work and composing. The field, the country is enormous, and many people are eager and willing to take hold. To many persons this movement has come like a new lease of life—a new and living interest.

This following constitutes a power not only in the direction of opening a way for the advance of composition, and the production of returns in membership, but in another and very important way for the future. It gives us an organ reaching and influencing people all over the country, who are going East and sending sons and daughters East to study.

It has long been my hope and expectation of building up a kind of Center, a kind of cooperative home, perhaps, where some of us could live and have it for a center of operations—where possibly a few persons could be accommodated who would be wishing to spend more or less time in or about Boston (many are doing this constantly), where they could receive musical instruction, where they would be drawn by the reputation of our work, where they would find an attractive musical *rendezvous.* From such a Center, we could make trips for organization, or recitals, or any purpose, as occasion demanded—in fact, plan such campaigns, just as I planned the campaign of this last month. Little by little we would bring about the necessary adjustments in our personal living arrangements, but meanwhile cooperating at the start, joining all forces, standing by each other for the maintenance of ourselves and those dependent upon us. My mother is eager for the accomplishing of such a thing, and would do much in the making of it an attractive center for artistic and intellectual people.

Now it seems to me, that the solution of your problem may find itself in just such a step. It would mean work, and fight, but you are a worker and a fighter through and through; but it would mean the building of a substantial basis for the future. The educational work would *not* of course be confined to *American music,* nor to pupils living in such a center.

My great need today, and for these years, is *Helpers*—helpers to organize.

I have had to leave the path I mapped out for myself (i.e., to be wholly on the literary and artistic side) for this absolute necessity for organization.

But I have had to carry on the artistic and literary work at the same time, which is too much, and to go on doing both (constantly at least) would be a menace to my health altogether too great to be contemplated. And it is particularly the organization work that I must recede from, because the literary work and general directing of the movement devolves necessarily on me, and others can organize exactly as well as I.

Also the organization work must go on, for in that lies the *realizing* of everything.

What I have learned by this unforeseen digression of mine, is *how to organize,* and that I can teach to others. In fact, the mere thought of myself alone being the only organizer for the United States—is absurd! Moreover, you will now have had the beginnings of experience in that direction. It is no more difficult to organize in a place where you are not previously known, than in your own place—in fact, I think it is easier. One carries a certain glamour coming from elsewhere, especially as the representative of a progressive movement. And the Wa-Wan is getting better and better known, and more and more credited.

It comes over me overwhelmingly that now is the moment of opportunity—these years, to unite and make a great reality of this work, which requires only that we make a common cause of it. I could not, at the present stage, pay you a living salary, were you to live elsewhere, or maintain a home elsewhere (that is, for organizing) but if we could all combine in some way, at Newton Center, say, and work in the common cause of mutual maintenance, at least until we could bring it further along, there is no reason why it could not be done, i.e. the work entered upon. What such living arrangements might be would have to be determined; a large house might be taken which would hold us all, or a small one besides ours, or extra rooms or apartments outside, with some plan for a common table.

Cooperation of some kind, of those having a similar need, seems to me the one way through. . . .

I have been working too hard, but it is through the *success of my method* that my eyes are opened to its possibilities as a practical way forward. And now, simply, I want others to join in carrying it out—where it can be of mutual helpfulness. . . .

Well think it over and write me soon—your impression—why we shouldn't join forces and do something. . . .

Ever faithfully yours,

Arthur Farwell

THE CHARM

APPENDIX D

Many of the devices discussed under "Methods," along with some others here mentioned for the first time, may be seen *in situ* in *The Charm* (1943).* I take them up in chronological order as they appear in the score.

Meas. 1: Signature, 3 flats. The changes of key signature in this work usually appear with double bars at changes of a text line. Meas. 39, however, has no double bar, which may have been an oversight. Meas. 29 restates the opening material with a new signature, probably chosen to fit the new continuation of the material. The piece swings to the flat side of C Minor after meas. 46, and about meas. 65 achieves the E-flat tonality of the ending.

Meas. 1–4: Harmonically the introduction is quite normal, with a drift of F to G roots over tonic pedal tones. At meas. 4 the accompaniment identifies the thematic motive that pervades most of the song.

Meas. 5–12: Quartal harmonies, rooted, with a common tone, C, which still continues as pedal.

Meas. 5–26: The vocal part is diatonic in two flats. The tonality is perhaps open to question. Some I believe will hear it in G, but for myself, overall, it lies in C minor. If that be true the melody is Dorian. The harmonic roots, largely C, E-flat, F, and G, can support either interpretation; but notice that the harmony, unlike the melody, is not diatonically modal.

Meas. 12–15: A passage built on characteristic tertian sonorities, augmented-minor sevenths on B-flat in meas. 12, E-flat in meas. 14. Note again that they harmonize a diatonic melody.

Meas. 16–20: Strength in E-flat major. This passage is the strongest threat to the primacy of C minor which, though it recurs briefly near the second section, gradually loses its influence over the long run of the song. The harmonies are chromatic and arranged within a powerful soprano-bass counterpoint.

Meas. 20–28: Reestablishment of C minor. Shepherd pens a gentle chordal alternation of F and A-flat roots, and a gradual return to quartal sonorities.

Meas. 29–32: Restatement of the beginning. The key signature is changed, as explained above.

Meas. 33–38: The melody outlines a diminished seventh chord, but is harmonized by a progression so utterly in conflict with that implication that it could go completely unnoticed. In view of Shepherd's attempts to avoid all manner and type of outmoded cliché his use of such an overworked chord may seem surprising. Such a melody, however, is always harmonized as we see here: with chords that subvert the harmonic implication of the melody. I believe these melodies resulted fortuitously from advanced harmonic thought, from a search for unexpected melodic tones in the key—in other words, from harmonic and melodic exploration of distant reaches of the key—rather than from an easy melodic conception that was later harmonized in a consciously elaborate and distracting fashion. But whichever be the case, the diminished seventh chord remained a part of Shepherd's melodic technique at all periods.

Meas. 33–34: The exploitation of chords related by common intervals is typical of Shepherd. The technique, though not the effect, is reminiscent of Scriabin's manipulations of his colorful chords. Here a major-minor-minor ninth on C alternates with a G-flat major triad with C pedal. If E-natural is understood throughout, only G-natural–G-flat differs between the two. The chord is changed through the operation of the thematic motive.

Meas. 37–38: The suddenness of the modulation is typical and is emphasized by a bit of text painting with the minor second D-sharp–E.

Meas. 39–45: A typical Shepherdian chromatic progression for a threatening subject or situation. The melody moves along a scale of alternating half- and whole steps, relating it closely to the diminished seventh melody discussed above. The harmonies exploit chromatic and cross relations, once again in the context of strong, two-voiced counterpoint in the outer parts. All leads to the surprising cadence at meas. 43. The connecting passage that follows is basically slippery chromaticism, heard in a creeping bass and subtle, implied, inner voice movements around C-sharp, C-natural, B-natural, C-natural.

Meas. 45–56: The melody continues along an artificial scale. The harmony settles into a gentle alternation of G-flat and E-flat roots. The last two notes of the solo ("may have") become a transition motive that, through a melodic alteration in meas. 55, achieves B-flat minor. This modulation is not only beautiful but admirable, for its harmonic ingenuity results from notes that are melodically and thematically inevitable.

Meas. 57–67: Aeolian mode on B-flat; pentatonic (or quartal) harmony initially, with a pedal tone throughout. The poet is speaking here, and no longer the sorcerer, whose magic seems to have failed. The last remaining hope is to invoke supernatural aid. The dancing with the fairies is perfectly diatonic. At the desperate plea, "melt her hard heart," however, Shepherd uses a marvelous F-flat to alter—to diffract, or distort—the harmony. Note again the fragment of the artificial scale in the melody at this hint of unnatural intervention. The passage is not unlike the drunken scene in *Invitation to the Dance.*

Meas. 67–68: The bass pedal tone magically changes to the dominant of E-flat, and at the double bar an utterly traditional progression, V-I, establishes a new key and a new situation.

Meas. 69–end: As the girl's mere glance dissolves all the occult spells woven about her, so this briefest reference to classic, tonal music, through its most common harmonic effect, is all that is needed to cast brilliant rays throughout the dark sorcerer's landscape in which we have been moving. Given Shepherd's personal style at this particular point in the history of the art, this passage is psychologically and dramatically perfect. Now the texture changes, the accompaniment motive drops out, and in typical love song music (actually, many of his songs are love songs) Shepherd throws his energy wholly into the musical depiction of a man's love for a beautiful girl. Meas. 70 finds him using the embellishing diminished seventh chord again, a sound that, often transformed into only an echo of the Romantic usage of his youth, rises unexpectedly out of the past in many of his mature works. At the end the whole tonality turns happily to the Lydian side of E-flat major.

NOTES

Notes, pp. 3–16

CHAPTER 1
PARIS TO BOSTON

1. Arthur Shepherd to William S. Newman, 27 December 1949, Arthur Shepherd Collection, Marriott Library of Fine Arts, University of Utah, Salt Lake City, Utah.

2. Ibid.

3. Jesse R. S. Budge, "Pioneer Days—Some Reminiscences," typescript, Shepherd Collection.

4. Joseph Russell Shepherd, "Birthplace and Early Environment," extract from Autobiography of Joseph Russell Shepherd, mimeographed, Shepherd Collection.

5. *Deseret News* (Salt Lake City), 1944 [exact date unknown].

6. Budge, "Pioneer Days."

7. Arthur Shepherd, interviews with the author.

8. Arthur Shepherd, "Biographical Sketch," manuscript, Shepherd Collection.

9. Budge, "Pioneer Days."

10. Arthur Shepherd to William S. Newman, 24 December 1949, Shepherd Collection.

11. Shepherd to Newman, 27 December 1949, Shepherd Collection.

12. Arthur Shepherd, "Orchestral Concerts for Children," *Journal of Proceedings of the Music Supervisors' National Conference* 16 (1923): 113–15.

13. Arthur Shepherd, "Papa Goetschius in Retrospect," *The Musical Quarterly* 30, no. 3 (July 1944): 307–18.

14. This collection is housed in the Marriott Library of Fine Arts, University of Utah, Salt Lake City, Utah.

15. Shepherd, "Papa Goetschius in Retrospect."

16. Shepherd to Newman, 24 December 1949, Shepherd Collection.

17. George D. Pyper, *The Romance of an Old Playhouse* (Salt Lake City: The Seagull Press, 1928), pp. 73, 77.

18. Shepherd to Newman, 24 December 1949, Shepherd Collection.

19. Bylaws of The American Music Society. For the complete bylaws see Richard N. Loucks, "Arthur Shepherd" (Ph.D. diss., Eastman School of Music of the University of Rochester, 1960), pp. 1115ff.

20. Interview with the author, 18 July 1953.

21. Farwell, at least, wrote letters of this kind (see Appendix C). I have been unable to locate Shepherd's side of the correspondence.

22. See Appendix C for the text of this letter dated "Nov. 20."

23. Probably September 1908.

24. Arthur Shepherd, "American Violin Music since 1876," *Volume of Proceedings of the Music Teachers National Association* 23 (1928): 220–26.

25. Arthur Farwell, "Toward American Music," *Transcript* (Boston), 20 May 1905.

26. Shepherd to Edward Waters, date unknown, Shepherd Collection.

27. Arthur Farwell, "Toward American Music."

28. Shepherd thought the decline of Farwell's and Gilbert's popularity could also be explained by a general change in musical aesthetics (the shift away from nationalism and romanticism). This change inevitably caught him along with them.

29. David Ewen, *American Composers Today* (New York: H. W. Wilson Co. 1949), p. 223.

30. Shepherd to Newman, 27 December 1969, Shepherd Collection.

31. A description of the conservatory in this period can be found in Allan Lincoln Langley, "Chadwick and the New England Conservatory of Music," *The Musical Quarterly* 21 (January 1935): 39–52.

32. Arthur Shepherd, "Harmonic Values—An Inquiry," *Volume of Proceedings of the Music Teachers National Association* 5 (1910): 115–23.

33. Arthur Shepherd, "American Music" (Lecture No. 2), manuscript, Shepherd Collection.

34. Arthur Shepherd, "American Music: The Traditionalists" (Lecture No. 1), manuscript, Shepherd Collection.

35. Shepherd to Edward Waters, date unknown, Shepherd Collection.

36. Shepherd to Newman, 24 December 1949, Shepherd Collection.

37. Shepherd then conducted the Cecilia Society for the 1917–18 seasons, following Chalmers Clifton. This position was terminated by his enlistment in the army.

38. The sonata bears a French title because it was published in Paris by Maurice Senart. It is possible that Loeffler's influence is also acknowledged here, for his music is French in spirit. In America the sonata is normally programmed under the title *Sonata for Pianoforte and Violin.*

39. Arthur Shepherd, "American Music" (Lecture No. 2), manuscript, Shepherd Collection.

40. Shepherd to Newman, 27 December 1949, Shepherd Collection.

41. In Cleveland, with the composer conducting.

42. Nikolai Sokoloff to Shepherd, 21 February 1920, Shepherd Collection. I assume that "Conservatory Project" refers to the Cleveland Institute of Music, which was founded in 1920 with Ernest Bloch as director.

CHAPTER 2
CLEVELAND

1. Arthur Shepherd, "Cleveland," in G. C. Sansoni, ed., *Enciclopedia dello spettacolo*, 9 vols. (Rome: Casa Editrice le Maschere, 1956), vol. 3, cols. 973–78. This quotation in English was taken from Shepherd's manuscript copy, now in the Arthur Shepherd Collection, Marriott Library of Fine Arts, University of Utah, Salt Lake City, Utah.

2. Home of the Cleveland Orchestra.

3. Grazella P. Shepherd to author, December 1967, Shepherd Collection.

4. Arthur Shepherd, "Orchestral Concerts for Children," *Journal of Proceedings of the Music Supervisors' National Conference* 16 (1923): 113–15.

5. Arthur Shepherd, "Cleveland Orchestra Program Notes," 4 and 6 November 1920, Huntington Library, San Marino, California.

6. Ibid., 24 and 26 April 1924.

7. Stanley S. Friedman, "Arthur Shepherd: Artist and Scholar," typescript, Shepherd Collection. [This article was written about 1931 for *The Musical Leader.*]

8. Grazella P. Shepherd to author, December 1967, Shepherd Collection.

9. Percy Goetschius to Arthur Shepherd, 16 January 1921, Shepherd Collection.

10. C. W. Morrison to Percy Goetschius, 29 March 1924, Shepherd Collection.

11. Percy Goetschius to Arthur Shepherd, 14 December 1924, Shepherd Collection.

12. Walter Willson Cobbett, *Cobbett's Cyclopedic Survey of Chamber Music,* ed. Colin Mason, 2d ed., 3 vols. (London: Oxford University Press, 1963), 1:49.

13. Ibid., p. 506.

14. Douglas Moore to Arthur Shepherd, 2 January 1950, Shepherd Collection.

15. Arthur Quimby to William S. Newman, 10 October 1949, Shepherd Collection.

16. According to Shepherd's recollections he resigned all duties with the orchestra in 1926. The information given here regarding his tenure with the orchestra is taken from the Program Notes of the Cleveland Orchestra.

17. The mark of a true patron is his willingness to encourage and support without controlling an artist. I did not know the Blossoms, but I have inferred that they met this definition of the patron from the following anecdote of Mrs. Shepherd: "We were Democrats and we lived through Roosevelt's election. Believe me, that was some accomplishment—because we lived with Republicans!" Grazella Shepherd to the author, December 1967.

18. Adella Prentiss Hughes. *Triptych* had been composed at her request. The program may be seen on page 20.

19. Grazella P. Shepherd to the author, December 1967, Shepherd Collection.

20. Ibid.

21. Ibid. Beryl Rubinstein died in 1952.

22. Ibid.

23. Arthur Shepherd to William S. Newman, 22 December 1949, Shepherd Collection.

CHAPTER 3
THE TEACHER

1. Grazella P. Shepherd to the author, December 1967, Arthur Shepherd Collection, Marriott Library of Fine Arts, University of Utah, Salt Lake City, Utah.

2. Karl Eschman, *Changing Forms in Modern Music* (Boston: E. C. Schirmer, 1945).

3. Ernest Toch, *The Shaping Forces in Music* (New York: Criterion Music Corp., 1948).

4. Arthur Shepherd, *The String Quartets of Ludwig van Beethoven* (Cleveland, Ohio: Horace Carr, 1935), p. ix.

5. Ibid.

6. Arthur Shepherd, interview with the author, 15 March 1956.

7. Ibid.

8. Arthur Shepherd, "Music in Higher Education," 1937, typescript, Shepherd Collection.

9. Ibid.; and "Types of Non-Professional Offerings," *Journal of Proceedings of the Music Supervisors' National Conference* 25 (1932): 194–97.

10. Arthur Shepherd, "Types of Non-Professional Offerings," p. 195.

11. See Tovey's remarks about "phrase by phrase" understanding of a work versus "*a priori* generalizations about form." Donald Francis Tovey, *Essays in Musical Analysis,* 5 vols. (London: Oxford University Press, 1935), vol. 1, *Symphonies,* p. 2.

12. Donald Francis Tovey, *Beethoven* (London: Oxford University Press, 1945), p. 111.

13. I once asked Shepherd who he remembered as talented students. His reply (and I hope no one was overlooked): William S. Newman,* James Aliferis, Starling Cumberworth,* Alvin Etler,* Vivien Harvey Slater, Eugene Weigh, Frederic Goosen, Lucy Browning, Theodore Chanler,* Paul Stofft, and Nathaniel Dett. (Conversation with author, 24 July 1954.) The asterisks indicate entries in Nicolas Slonimsky, ed., *Baker's Biographical Dictionary of Musicians,* 6th ed. (New York: Schirmer, 1978).

14. Knud Jeppesen, *Counterpoint,* trans. Glen Haydon (New York: Prentice-Hall, 1939).

15. Arthur Tillman Merritt, *Sixteenth-Century Polyphony* (Cambridge, Mass.: Harvard University Press, 1949).

16. By "applied music" I denote the study of voice or an instrument as a part of the curriculum of a college or university.

CHAPTER 4
THOUGHTS ABOUT MUSIC

1. Jules Combarieu, *Music: Its Laws and Evolution* (London: Kegan, Paul, Trench, Trubner & Co., 1910), p. 29.

2. Donald Francis Tovey, *Beethoven* (London: Oxford University Press, 1944), p. 45: "To great composers, music is neither a game nor a science, but a language. . . ."

3. Arthur Shepherd, "Introduction to Lecture 1," manuscript, Arthur Shepherd Collection, Marriott Library of Fine Arts, University of Utah, Salt Lake City, Utah.

4. Shepherd, "Types of Non-Professional Offerings," *Volume of Proceedings of the Music Supervisors' National Conference* 25 (1932): 194–97.

5. W. H. Hadow, *Collected Essays* (London: Oxford University Press, 1928), p. 197.

6. Shepherd, "Fashions, Survivals and Vitality in Contemporary Music: The Goings On and Happenings in Music," 1 March 1954, Museum lecture, Shepherd Collection.

7. Shepherd, "Franz Schubert," lecture for the Institute (probably The Cleveland Institute of Music), Shepherd Collection.

8. BAch, HAYdn, MOzart, BEEthoven, SCHUBert.

9. Albert Schweitzer.

10. Oswald Spengler.

11. Pitirim Sorokin.

12. Shepherd to William S. Newman, 24 December 1949, Shepherd Collection.

13. Shepherd, "American Music" (Lecture No. 2), manuscript, Shepherd Collection.

14. Paul Hindemith, *The Craft of Musical Composition: Book I, Theoretical Part,* tr. Arthur Mendel (New York: Associated Music Publishers, 1942), p. 4.

15. Shepherd, "Wit in Music," lecture, Shepherd Collection. Note also this remark from Shepherd's letter to Newman, 24 December 1949: "But mind you, I am *not* by *training* or *inclination* either philosopher or aesthetician. I am more interested in history and *theory;* but not the sort of pseudo analytical theory that the aestheticians wallow around in."

16. Shepherd, "Notes for a Class in Cleveland," 1953, manuscript, Shepherd Collection.

17. Conversation with the author.

18. Shepherd, "American Music" (Lecture No. 2), manuscript, Shepherd Collection.

19. Shepherd, Sketchbook, Shepherd Collection.

20. Arthur Shepherd, "Tradition," from "American Music" Lecture No. 1, manuscript, Shepherd Collection.

21. Conversation with the author.

22. Arnold Schoenberg, "Brahms the Progressive," *Style and Idea,* trans. Dika Newlin (London: Williams & Norgate, 1951), pp. 52–101.

23. Shepherd's statement continued: "for example the passage in the E minor Quartet before letter M [in the third movement:]

This tune affinity is, obviously, reflected in other works: Fantasia on Down East Spirituals, and the Fantasia on 'the Garden Hymn.' I suppose also that the jig variation (IV) in the [Second] Sonata might be the dance counterpart of the same spirit."

24. William S. Newman, "Arthur Shepherd," *The Musical Quarterly* 36 (April 1950): 159–79.

25. Shepherd to the author, 10 January 1957, Shepherd Collection.

26. Shepherd, "Franz Schubert," manuscript, Shepherd Collection.

27. Conversation with the author.

28. Roger Sessions, *The Musical Experience* (Princeton, N.J.: Princeton University Press, 1950), p. 54.

29. He included the scherzo. Conversation with the author.

30. Rudoph Reti, *The Thematic Process in Music* (New York: Macmillan Co., 1951).

31. Conversation with the author.

32. Ibid.

33. See also pages 38 and 39.

34. Shepherd was hard of hearing in his later years.

35. "To approach Her Honor *again*," he might well have said. At his request Judge Florence Ellinwood Allen had already added a few lines to the poem in order to give him more room to turn around in.

36. Shepherd to the author, 9 December 1955.

37. Denoe Leedy, "American Composers XV: Arthur Shepherd," *Modern Music* 16, no. 2 (January-February 1939): 87–93.

38. Ibid., p. 89.

39. Ibid.

40. See pages 41–42.

41. Arthur Loesser, "Symphony No. 2 in D Minor [by] Arthur Shepherd—"Cleveland Orchestra Program Notes" (Twenty-Second Season, 1939–1940), 7–9 March 1940, Huntington Library, San Marino, California.

42. See pages 44–45.

CHAPTER 5 WORDS AND MUSIC

1. Arthur Shepherd, conversation with the author.

2. James Joyce, *Chamber Music*, (New York: B. W. Huebsch, 1918). "Who goes amid the green wood" is poem 8; "Winds of May" is poem 9.

3. The complete list of Shepherd's poets may be seen in Appendix B.

4. Oliver St. John Gogarty, "Virgil," in *Others to Adorn* (London: Rich & Cowan, 1938).

5. Arthur Shepherd to the author, 17 February 1955.

6. Page 34.

7. *The Truants* (1945), p. 2; *In the Scented Bud of the Morning** (1941), p. 3.

8. *Softly Along the Road of Evening, Virgil, In the Scented Bud of the Morning,* Serenade* (1949), *The Word, Heart's Journey,* Sarasvati* (1957).*

9. *Oh, Like a Queen's Her Happy Tread,* Most Quietly at Times,* The Starling Lake;* also, but freer in form, "Light, My Light" from *Triptych, Where Loveliness Keeps House,* Golden Stockings, Spring Duet* (1942),* *The Truants.**

10. *The Gentle Lady,* Sunday up the River,* To a Trout* (1941), *The Charm* (1943),* "He It Is" from *Triptych.*

11. *When Rooks Fly Homeward,* A Ballad of Trees and the Master* (in which the correspondence of sections is due to a refrain).

12. *Bacchus,* Invitation to the Dance, The Fiddlers.*

13. *Sun Down,** "He It Is" and "Light, My Light" from *Triptych.*

14. Goetschius's term to denote the process of preparing for a recapitulation.

15. Measure 54: The original motive is used, but not fulfilled as at the beginning.

16. *Deck Thyself My Soul* (1918), *Carol* (1940).

CHAPTER 6 ARTISTIC MATURITY

1. Cleveland Orchestra conducted by Arthur Shepherd, 7 and 9 March 1940.

2. Boston Symphony Orchestra conducted by Arthur Shepherd, season of 1940.

3. Arthur Shepherd to William S. Newman, 22 December 1949, Arthur Shepherd Collection, Marriott Library of Fine Arts, University of Utah, Salt Lake City, Utah.

4. Grazella P. Shepherd to the author, December 1967, Shepherd Collection.

5. Arthur Shepherd, "Papa Goestschius in Retrospect," *The Musical Quarterly* 30 (1944): 312.

6. Ibid.

7. Beryl Rubinstein.

8. Dudley Blossom.

9. The Richmond Road house, built for the Shepherds by the Blossoms, had to be sold in settling the estate.

10. On Lennox Road, in Cleveland Heights.

11. "Padre's garden . . . a sort of loved wellbeing, rather than a groomed garden where things are commanded, not just permitted, to grow. (It had no weeds though!)" Grazella P. Shepherd to the author, 15 February 1968, Shepherd Collection.

12. Peter Shepherd, their son.

13. Dr. William B. Seymour.

14. Grazella P. Shepherd to the author, December 1967, Shepherd Collection.

15. Manfred Bukofzer, musicologist. In 1942 he joined the faculty of the University of California at Berkeley, where he remained until his death in 1955.

16. Arthur Quimby to William S. Newman, 10 October 1949, Shepherd Collection.

17. Shepherd to Newman, 20 December 1949, Shepherd Collection.

18. Shepherd to Newman, 4 June 1950, Shepherd Collection.

19. Shepherd to Newman, 11 May 1950, Shepherd Collection.

20. See page 54.

21. Olin Downes, music critic of the *New York Times. Triptych* was performed on May 20, 1950 in the second concert of the Sixth Annual Festival of Contemporary American Music, given under the sponsorship of the Alice M. Ditson Fund of Columbia University. Four works were performed, by Edward Burlingame Hill, Arthur Shepherd, and two younger composers. Downes wrote, "At the risk of being consigned to the doghouse which is inhabited by the 'Conservatives,' or even worse the 'romantics,' we are prone to remark that on this occasion the older man came out considerably better than the young. Such, at least, is our conclusion. . . . Mr. Shepherd's settings of the poetry of Tagore are among the best music we know that has come from his pen. He has written with spontaneity and lyrical fervor, and a highly perceptive treatment of his text. The three poems which make his Triptych offer sufficient variety of mood to afford essential contrasts, while on the other hand the unity of the textual and musical conception is impressive. The part of the string quartet is not merely one of accompaniment. It has melodic impulse and polyphony as well as harmonic sensitiveness. The songs were admirably interpreted by Marie Kraft and the playing of the New Music String Quartet was another of the composer's fortunate assets."

22. Shepherd to Newman, 4 June 1950, Shepherd Collection. The New York performance was by Marie Simmelink Kraft and the New Music Quartet.

23. William S. Newman, "Arthur Shepherd," *The Musical Quarterly* 36 (April 1950): 159–79.

24. Shepherd to Newman, 30 October 1949, Shepherd Collection.

25. Paul Henry Lang, editor, and Nathan Broder, associate editor, of *The Musical Quarterly.*

26. Shepherd to Newman, 11 May 1950, Shepherd Collection.

27. *Piano Music of Arthur Shepherd* (Vivien Harvey Slater, pianist), published and copyrighted by Western Reserve University, 1967, LCN 67-3434.

28. Dr. Jerome Gross, surgeon and violinist.

29. *Songs of Arthur Shepherd* (Marie Simmelink Kraft, mezzo-soprano; Marianne Matousek Mastics, piano), published by the Department of Music of Western Reserve University, ca. 1960.

30. Grazella P. Shepherd to the author, December 1967, Shepherd Collection.

31. Grazella P. Shepherd to the author, December 1967, Shepherd Collection.

32. Grazella P. Shepherd to Newman, 12 December 1949, Shepherd Collection.

33. Grazella P. Shepherd to the author, December 1967, Shepherd Collection.

34. Ibid.

35. A radio commentator.

36. Grazella P. Shepherd to the author, December 1967, Shepherd Collection.

37. See Appendix A. There are two catalogs.

CHAPTER 7 BOSTON STYLE

1. Daniel Gregory Mason, ed., *The Art of Music: A Comprehensive Library of Information for Music Lovers and Musicians* (New York: National Society of Music,

1915), vol. 4, *Music in America*, ed. Arthur Farwell and W. Dermot Darby, p. 417.

2. Richard N. Loucks, "Arthur Shepherd" (Ph.D. diss., Eastman School of Music of the University of Rochester, 1960), chapters 7–9. This summary is based on an analysis of twenty works written between 1913 and 1951.

3. See page 63.

4. Because of the numerous accidentals in Shepherd's early music, one may wonder why I so often describe it as basically diatonic in conception. When accidentals occur as the result of modulation (extended or transient), as harmonic embellishment of common progressions (secondary dominants and borrowed chords), as part of the momentary alteration of a scale by the characteristic tones of another mode or scale, and so on, I recognize an underlying, if shifting, diatonic foundation to the tonality. In this book I shall reserve the term "chromaticism" for situations in which semitonal creeping (in the form of the alteration of a letter name—C-C-sharp, for example) is the predominant harmonic or melodic principle. A comparison of Bach's *Chromatische Fantasie und Fuga* (which is basically diatonic by the criteria here given) with the same composer's *Das alte Jahr vergangen ist* or Richard Wagner's *Tristan und Isolde* should make this distinction clear.

5. For a description of the tuneful nature of many of Shepherd's melodies see page 33.

6. Arthur Shepherd to William S. Newman, 21 December 1949, Arthur Shepherd Collection, Marriott Library of Fine Arts, University of Utah, Salt Lake City, Utah.

7. Shepherd to Newman, 22 December 1949, Shepherd Collection.

CHAPTER 8
THE CLEVELAND STYLE

1. Relative to the major and minor scales the Dorian is a natural minor scale with the sixth tone raised by a chromatic half-step (sharp 6); the Phrygian is a natural minor scale with flat 2; the Lydian is a major scale with sharp 4; and the Mixolydian is a major scale with flat 7.

2. Modal melodies: *Two Step;* Eclogue No. 1.** Modal chords: *In the Scented Bud of the Morning,** meas. 9; *Bacchus,** meas. 86–87; *Softly along the Road of Evening,* meas. 7, 27.

3. References to modal writing:

Dorian: *Reverie.**

Phrygian: *Second Sonata,* first subject and meas. 19–22; *Sonata for Pianoforte and Violin,* first subject and meas. 173–76.

Lydian: *Two Step;* Song of the Pilgrims,* p. 2; *Morning Glory; Golden Stockings; In the Scented Bud of the Morning,** meas. 39–end; *Sonata for Pianoforte and Violin,* third movement.

Mixolydian: *Matin Song;* Second Sonata,* first movement, p. 5 at "soave"; also theme of second movement.

Mixed modes: *Second Sonata,* "Toccata"; *Most Quietly at Times,** meas. 37–44; *In the Scented Bud of the Morning,** melody meas. 1–4.

4. References to tertian chords:

Diminished triads: *The Gentle Lady,** meas. 20; *Morning Glory,* meas. 17; *When Rooks Fly Homeward,** meas. 57–58.

Augmented triads: *Oh, Like a Queen's Her Happy Tread,** meas. 8; *Invitation to the Dance,* p. 1, score 4; also p. 9, score 1; *Morning Glory,* meas. 51.

Minor seventh chord (minor triad plus minor seventh): *Invitation to the Dance,* p. 7; *Nocturne,** meas. 26; *Bacchus,** meas. 21, 52.

Major seventh chord (major triad plus major seventh): *Capriccio No. 1,** meas. 13; *Invitation to the Dance,* p. 1; *Exotic Dance No. 2,** meas. 2; *Processionale Festivo,** meas. 2; *Morning Glory,* meas. 2.

Half-diminished seventh chord (diminished triad plus minor seventh): *Nocturne,** meas. 38; *In the Scented Bud of the Morning,** meas. 27–30.

Augmented sixth chords: *The Gentle Lady,** meas. 8, 27; *Invitation to the Dance,* p. 10, score 2; *Quintet for Pianoforte and Strings,* second movement, meas. 115–21.

Augmented major seventh (augmented triad plus major seventh: *Exotic Dance No. 2,** meas. 65–74; *Prelude* (G Minor), meas. 17; *The Charm,** meas. 12–15.

Diminished major seventh (diminished triad plus major seventh): *Eclogue No. 3,** meas. 57 (enharmonic spelling); *Processionale Festivo,** meas. 15.

Various tall tertian chords: *Eclogue No. 1,** meas. 20–33; *Scherzino,** meas. 7–8; *In the Scented Bud of the Morning,** meas. 37; *The Truants,** meas. 45–50; *Bacchus,** meas. 87; *Eclogue No. 3,** last chord.

5. In one analysis of some twenty works as many as a sixth of the sonorities were tertian chords with added tones. See Richard N. Loucks, "Arthur Shepherd" (Ph.D. diss., Eastman School of Music of the University of Rochester, 1960).

6. Typical added tone chords; except as labeled "dissonant bass tones" all these examples are of added tones in the upper parts.

Major triad plus augmented fourth: *Eclogue No. 1,** meas. 56; *Eclogue No. 3,** meas. 22; *The Charm,** meas. 21, 23.

Major triad plus major sixth: *Scherzino,** meas. 110; *Where Loveliness Keeps House,** meas. 22; *Morning Glory,* meas. 6.

Major triad plus major ninth: *Eclogue No. 1,** meas. 41–43; *Nocturne,** meas. 52; *Scherzino,** meas. 117; *Invitation to the Dance,* p. 2 at C; *When Rooks Fly Homeward,** meas. 30–32.

Major triad plus augmented fourth and major sixth: *Bacchus,** meas. 4, 7.

Major triad plus major sixth and major ninth: *Nocturne,** meas. 25; *Where Loveliness Keeps House,** meas. 1.

Minor triad plus augmented fourth: *Prelude* (G Minor),* meas. 1; *Eclogue No. 3,** meas. 55.

Minor triad plus minor sixth: *Exotic Dance No. 2,** last chord.

Minor triad plus major sixth: *Scherzino,** last chord.

Minor triad plus augmented fourth and major sixth: *Two Step,** meas. 157.

Minor triad plus major sixth and major ninth (or half-diminished seventh plus perfect fourth): *Two Step,** meas. 38.

Major minor seventh plus minor third: *Capriccio No. 1,** meas. 54.

Minor major seventh plus augmented fourth: *Eclogue No. 1,** meas. 52.

Chords with dissonant bass tones: *Capriccio No. 1,** meas. 60; *Nocturne,** meas. 88–91; *Where Loveliness Keeps House,** meas. 14–16; *Spinning Song,** meas. 61–62; *Invitation to the Dance,* p. 2 at C.

7. Suspensions: *When Rooks Fly Homeward,** meas. 15, 24, 25; "Light, My Light," meas. 30, from *Triptych; A Ballad of Trees and the Master,* p. 9.

8. Pedal tones: *Invitation to the Dance,* pp. 4–5, I through K; *Most Quietly at Times,** p. 3, meas. 2; *Sunday up the River;* Reverie,** meas. 1–22; *Softly Along the Road of Evening,* meas. 1–13.

9. Nonharmonic melodies: *Processionale Festivo,** meas. 30–31; *Quartet for Strings in E Minor,* p. 3 at *Piu tranquillo.*

10. See also *Scherzino,** p. 4, meas. 109–18.

11. See also *Fantasia on "The Garden Hymn"* (organ version), p. 14 at *Giubilante.*

12. Copyright 1929 by the Juilliard Musical Foundation. Reduction to piano score by Richard N. Loucks.

13. Chordal alternation: *Eclogue No. 1,** meas. 37–43; *Bacchus,** meas. 31–45.

14. Chordal alternation: *Where Loveliness Keeps House,** meas. 1–8; *Second Sonata,* first movement, meas. 23–28; "Light, My Light" at A (full score, p. 17, meas. 19–22, from *Triptych; Overture to a Drama,* p. 53.

15. Change of mode modulation: *Sun Down,** p. 1 at "There falls . . ."

Common tone modulations: *Spring Duet,** p. 3 at "Spring is it you . . ."; *Morning Glory,* meas. 26–29; *In the Scented Bud of the Morning,** meas. 31.

Common chord and common tone: *When Rooks Fly Homeward,** meas. 30; *Where Loveliness Keeps House,** meas. 32–33.

Altered common chord: *The Truants,** last phrase and final cadence; *The Gentle Lady,** meas. 22–24, 32–33.

Non-tertian common chord: *Horizons,* p. 6, meas. 4; p. 16, meas. 7.

16. Modulation by form: *The Song of the Pilgrims,* pp. 7–8 at M.

17. *Softly Along the Road of Evening,* meas. 24–26 at "fold" (note "common tone," C natural); *Oh, Like a Queen's Her Happy Tread,** meas. 28–30 at "free . . ." (chromatic modulation).

18. Chromatic modulations: *Virgil,* last vocal phrase at "tomb"; *Nocturne,** meas. 39–40, 74–75, 82–83; *Matin Song,** meas. 71–72 at "Sing my fair love . . ."; *When Rooks Fly Homeward,** meas. 25–31.

19. Melodic identification of the new key: *In Modo Ostinato,* meas. 32–33 at the double bar; *Processionale Festivo,** meas. 23–24; *Most Quietly at Times,** meas. 28–29 at "And suddenly . . ." *Eclogue* (Presser, 1948), meas. 13. G-flat is introduced. Note the increasing importance of this tone, resulting in the modulation to F-sharp minor at *Poco piu mosso.* Then see the reverse process, beginning in meas. 28, with the introduction of A-flat/G-sharp, which results in the modulation to G-sharp minor at the next double bar. The change to the tonic major occurs in meas. 45–46 by change of mode and enharmonic notation. Of interest also are the harmonics in meas. 8–11 and 27–28.

20. Loucks, "Arthur Shepherd," p. 1059.

21. Arthur Shepherd to Percy Goetschius, 6 November 1934, Arthur Shepherd Collection, Marriott Library of Fine Arts, University of Utah, Salt Lake City, Utah.

22. Shepherd, Sketchbook No. 18, Shepherd Collection.

23. Polychord: *Spinning Song,** meas. 63–66.

24. Whole-tone music will be found in *The City in the Sea, Song of the Sea Wind,* the Violin Sonata, the Second Piano Sonata, and *Processionale Festivo,* meas. 76. The clearest published example appears in Horizons, p. 11.

25. See also the end of *Spinning Song.**

26. Non-tertian and quartal passages: *Fantasia on "The Garden Hymn"; Jolly Wat; Morning Glory,* meas. 7–10; *Invitation to the Dance,* opening choral passage; *Eclogue No. 1,** meas. 15–16, 44, 86–87; *Capriccio No. 1,** meas. 4, 9, 15–16, 22; *Two Step,** meas. 148; *Exotic Dance No. 2,** meas. 9–10; *Scherzino,** meas. 82, 85,

89; *Capriccio No. 3,** meas. 55–56, 67; *Eclogue No. 3,** meas. 29–30; *Bacchus,** meas. 31, 58–61; *The Charm,** meas. 6–11.

27. Long sonorities: *Nocturne,** meas. 59–67; "The Day Is No More," beginning and end, from *Triptych; Lento Amabile,* meas. 35–41; *Capriccio No. 1,** meas. 68–71; *Two Step,** meas. 67–74.

28. *Exotic Dance No. 1,** beginning.

29. Melodic use of an artificial scale of alternating whole and half-steps: *Capriccio No. 2,* meas. 77–78; *Quintet for Pianoforte and Strings,* first movement, meas. 84–86; *The Fiddlers,* meas. 59–63; *Virgil,* meas. 42–43, 49–50; *The Truants,** meas. 25–27; *Where Loveliness Keeps House,** meas. 32–33.

Melodic use of diminished seventh chords: "He It Is," meas. 40–48, from *Triptych;* "Light, My Light," meas. 34–40, from *Triptych; Invitation to the Dance,* pp. 12–13; *Two Step,** meas. 35–38; *Processionale Festivo,** meas. 32–37, 63–64; *Morning Glory,* meas. 16–20; *Serenade,* meas. 31–32. See also the analysis of *The Charm,* meas. 33–38, in Appendix D.

30. *Quintet for Pianoforte and Strings.*

31. James Aliferis, formerly a student of Shepherd at Western Reserve University, composer and professor of music at the University of Minnesota, where he had performed the *Invitation to the Dance.*

32. Shepherd to William S. Newman, 21 December 1949.

33. Traditional counterpoint: *Autumn Fields,* beginning; *Souvenir;* Psalm XLII,* p. 15.

34. See pages 52, 57.

35. Non-traditional counterpoint: *Quintet for Pianoforte and Strings,* p. 41; *Quartet for Strings No. 4,* p. 9, meas. 128, and the beginning of the third movement; *Quartet for Strings in E Minor,* second movement; *Eclogue No. 2; Capriccio No. 3;** *Most Quietly at Times.**

36. Newman to the author, personal communication, n.d.

37. By "inversion" I refer to the inversion (switching) of parts in double counterpoint, not to contrary motion of one or more parts.

38. Compare meas. 29–32 with 130–34. This device is seldom used, taught, or for that matter even written about. See discussion of "inversion by contrary motion" in H. C. Colles, ed., *Grove's Dictionary of Music and Musicians,* 3d ed., 5 vols. (New York: St. Martin's Press, 1927), 3:723; or "melodic inversion" in Eric Blom, ed., *Grove's Dictionary of Music and Musicians,* 5th ed., 9 vols. (New York: St. Martin's Press, 1954), 2:479.

39. Doubled melodies in piano writing: *Matin Song,** beginning; *Capriccio No. 2,* p. 8; *Second Sonata,* p. 4, 12–13; *Scherzino,** meas. 79–83, 107–8; *Golden Stockings,* meas. 33–34.

40. Pianistic motive development: *Virgil; Exotic Dance No. 2;** *Exotic Dance No. 3.**

41. See page 52.

42. At one time Shepherd planned to reduce these extra forces, but I am not aware that he carried out his intention.

43. George H. L. Smith, "Cleveland Orchestra Program Notes," 9 and 11 April 1953, Huntington Library, San Marino, California.

44. Sonata forms: *Overture to a Drama; Sonata for Pianoforte and Violin,* first and second movements; *Quartet for Strings in E Minor,* first movement; *Symphony No. 2,* first movement; *Concerto for Violin and Orchestra,* first movement.

45. Sonata-rondo mixtures: "Westward," from *Horizons; Quartet for Strings No. 4,* first and third movements; *Capriccio No. 1;** *Capriccio No. 3.**

46. Denoe Leedy, "American Composers XV: Arthur Shepherd," *Modern Music* 16, no. 2 (January-February 1939): 87–93.

SELECTIVE BIBLIOGRAPHY

SELECTIVE BIBLIOGRAPHY

This bibliography does not include all the sources referred to in the footnotes, nor does it contain books of only general application. Rather, it is a list of letters, manuscripts, articles, books, and other materials useful to those especially interested in Arthur Shepherd's life and music. The primary materials for this study were Shepherd's scores, files, and library, all of which are now housed as the Arthur Shepherd Collection in the Marriott Library of Fine Arts of the University of Utah, Salt Lake City, Utah.

Budge, Jesse R. S. "Pioneer Days—Some Reminiscences." Typescript. Shepherd Collection.

Case, Gilbert. *America's Music.* New York: McGraw-Hill, 1955.

Cleveland *Commercial.* 16 December 1922. Article on children's concerts of the Cleveland Orchestra. [Reprinted in "Cleveland Orchestra Program Notes." 4 and 6 January 1923. Huntington Library, San Marino, California.]

Cobbett, Walter Willson. *Cobbett's Cyclopedic Survey of Chamber Music.* 2 vols. London: Oxford University Press, 1929. 2d ed (3 vols.). Ed. Colin Mason. London: Oxford University Press, 1963.

Cooley, Everett L.; Dye, Della L.; and Ward, Margery W. "Register of the Papers of Arthur Shepherd (1880–1958)." Mimeographed. Salt Lake City: Special Collections Department, University of Utah Libraries, 1978.

Cutter, Benjamin. *Harmonic Analysis.* Boston: O. Ditson; New York: C. H. Ditson, 1902.

Elwell, Herbert. "Elwell Restates Case for Unprejudiced Consideration of American Conductor." Cleveland *Plain Dealer.* 28 February 1943.

Ewen, David. *American Composers Today.* New York: H. W. Wilson Co., 1949.

Farwell, Arthur. Letters to Arthur Shepherd. Ca. 1905–47. Shepherd Collection.

______. "Toward American Music." Offprint from the Boston *Transcript.* 20 May 1905.

______. *Home Life and Music Study: Announcement of Mr. Arthur Farwell and Mr. Arthur Shepherd.* Newton Center, Mass.: n.p., 1908–9.

______, and W. Dermot Darby. "Arthur Shepherd." *Music in America.* The Art of Music, ed. Daniel Gregory Mason, vol. 4. New York: The National Society of Music, 1915.

Farwell, Brice, ed. *A Guide to the Music of Arthur Farwell and to the Microfilm Collection of His Work.* Briarcliff Manor, New York: n.p., 1972.

Friedman, Stanley. "Arthur Shepherd: Artist and Scholar." Typescript article. Shepherd Collection. [Originally written for *The Musical Leader,* 1931.]

Gilbert, Henry F. Letters to Arthur Shepherd. 1905–11. Shepherd Collection.

Goetschius, Percy. Letters to Arthur Shepherd. Ca. 1905–42. Shepherd Collection.

Hindemith, Paul. *A Composer's World.* Cambridge, Mass.: Harvard University Press, 1952.

______. *The Craft of Musical Composition.* Trans. by Arthur Mendel. Vol. 1. New York: Associated Music Publishers, 1942.

Howard, John Tasker. *Our American Music.* New York: Thomas Y. Crowell, 1948.

______. *Our Contemporary Composers.* New York: Thomas Y. Crowell, 1941.

Hughes, Adella Prentiss. *Music Is My Life.* Cleveland, Ohio: World Publishing Co., 1947.

Kennedy, Charles E. *Fifty Years of Cleveland: 1875–1925.* Cleveland, Ohio: Weidenthall, 1925.

Langley, Allan Lincoln. "Chadwick and the New England Conservatory of Music." *The Musical Quarterly* 21 (January 1935): 39–52.

Leedy, Denoe. "American Composers XV: Arthur Shepherd." *Modern Music,* 16, no. 2 (January-February 1939): 87–93.

Letters to Arthur Shepherd. Ca. 1900–1958. Shepherd Collection. [The composer's correspondence included many prominent American musicians.]

Loesser, Arthur. *"Horizons . . ."* "Cleveland Orchestra Program Notes." 19 and 21 December 1929. Huntington Library, San Marino, California.

———. *"Symphony No. 2 . . ."* "Cleveland Orchestra Program Notes." 7 and 9 March 1940. Huntington Library, San Marino, California.

Loucks, Richard Newcomb. "Arthur Shepherd." Ph.D. dissertation, Eastman School of Music of the University of Rochester, 1960. Microcard publication: Rochester, N.Y.: University of Rochester Press, 1962. [This work contains photographic facsimilies and microfilms of most of Arthur Shepherd's manuscripts.]

———. "The Arthur Shepherd Collection." Mimeographed. Cleveland, Ohio: Freiberger Library, Western Reserve University, 1958. [Original in Shepherd Collection.]

McDermott, William F. "McDermott on Rodzinski." Cleveland *Plain Dealer.* c. 23 February 1943.

Newman, William S. "Arthur Shepherd." *Musical Quarterly* 36 (April 1950): 159–79.

———. Review of *Triptych for High Voice and String Quartet,* by Arthur Shepherd, as performed by Marie Kraft and the Walden String Quartet. *The Musical Quarterly* 39 (July 1953): 496–97.

———. *The Pianist's Problems.* 2d ed. New York: Harper, 1974.

Programs of all performances, public and private. Shepherd Collection.

Program of the Fine Arts Program of Western Reserve University. *"The Mother of Us All* by Virgil Thomson." 18 and 19 February 1949. Shepherd Collection.

Pyper, George D. *The Romance of an Old Playhouse.* Salt Lake City, Utah: The Seagull Press, 1926.

Reis, Clare. *Composers in America.* New York: Macmillan Co., 1947.

Schoenberg, Arnold. *Style and Idea.* Trans. by Dika Newlin. London: Williams & Norgate, 1951.

Sessions, Roger. *The Musical Experience of Composer, Performer, Listener.* Princeton, N.J.: Princeton University Press, 1950.

Shepherd, Arthur. Musical compositions and prose works, both published and in manuscript, are listed in Appendix A.

Shepherd, Grazella P. Voice letter (tape recording) to Richard Loucks. December 1967. Shepherd Collection.

Shepherd, Joseph Russell. "Birthplace and Early Environment." Extract from Autobiography of Joseph Russell Shepherd. Mimeographed. Shepherd Collection.

Slonimsky, Nicolas, ed. *Baker's Biographical Dictionary of Musicians.* 6th ed. New York: Schirmer, 1978.

———. *Music Since 1900,* 4th ed. New York: Charles Scribner's Sons, 1971.

Smith, George H. L. *"Theme and Variations . . .",* "Cleveland Orchestra Program Notes." 9 and 11 April 1953. Huntington Library, San Marino, California.

Western Reserve University. "The Little Broadside: A Bibliography of the Works of Dr. Arthur Shepherd, Professor of Music, Western Reserve University to November 1949." Mimeographed. Cleveland, Ohio: Western Reserve University Libraries, 1949.

INDEX

A

B

C

D

E

F

G

H

I

J

K

L

M

N

O

P

Q

R

S

T

U

V

W